Richard G. Beauchamp

Bichon Frise

Everything about Purchase, Care, Nutrition,
Breeding, Behavior, and Training

with over 30 Color and Black and White Photographs

Illustrations by Michele Earle-Bridges

BARRON'S

About the Author

Richard G. Beauchamp has been a lifelong dog breeder and exhibitor. He has judged all breeds of purebred dogs in every major country of the world and written about dogs and dog breeding for publications in many countries including Australia, England and America. He was instrumental in achieving American Kennel Club recognition of the bichon frise and participated in writing the American Kennel Club breed standard. Under the Beau Monde kennel prefix he has bred seventy American Kennel Club champions, many of them holding impressive Variety Group and Best In Show honors.

Photo Credits

John Ashbey: pages 8, 13 (top left); Barbara Augello: pages 44, 49, 81; Susan Green: cover, pages 53, 56, 57, 60 (top and bottom); Lawrence: pages 20, 21, 28; Don Petrulis: page 13 (bottom); Judith E. Strom: pages 29, 41, 85, 92 (top and bottom), 93; Missy Yuhl: inside front cover, inside back cover, back cover, pages 4, 12, 17, 23, 24, 40, 51, 61, 73, 76.

All inquiries should be addressed to:
Barron's Educational Series, Inc.
250 Wireless Boulevard
Hauppauge, NY 11788

International Standard Book No. 0-8120-9465-4

Library of Congress Catalog Card No. 95-39596

Library of Congress Cataloging-in-Publication Data
Beauchamp, Richard G.
    Bichon frise : everything about purchase, care, nutrition, breeding, behavior, and training / Richard G. Beauchamp.
        p. cm. — (A complete pet owner's manual)
    Includes bibliographical references (p.).
    ISBN 0-8120-9465-4
    1. Bichon frise. I. Title. II. Series.
SF429.B52B43   1996
636.7′2—dc20   95-39596
                                            CIP

Printed in Hong Kong

13 12 11 10 9 8 7 6 5 4 3

Important Notes

This pet owner's guide tells the reader how to buy and care for a bichon frise. The author and the publisher consider it important to point out that the advice given in the book primarily concerns normally developed puppies from a good breeder—that is, dogs of excellent physical health and good character.

Anyone who adopts a fully grown dog should be aware that the animal has already formed its basic impressions of human beings. The new owner should watch the animal carefully, including its behavior toward humans, and should meet the previous owner. If the dog comes from a shelter, it may be possible to get some information on the dog's background and peculiarities there. Some dogs, as a result of bad experiences with humans, behave in an unnatural manner or may even bite. Only people that have experience with dogs should take in such animals.

Caution is further advised in the association of children with dogs, in meeting with other dogs, and in exercising the dog without a leash.

Even well-behaved and carefully supervised dogs sometimes do damage to someone else's property or cause accidents. It is therefore in the owner's interest to be adequately insured against such eventualities, and we strongly urge all dog owners to purchase a liability policy that covers their dog.

Contents

The bichon is right at home in any setting.

Preface

Dogs, purebred and otherwise, have been an important part of my life since early childhood. While still a preschool youngster, I spent many happy hours with an uncle who raised setters and beagles for the field. This was my introduction to dog care and training.

Since then I have bred and exhibited dogs of many different breeds, each with its own distinct personality and character. In 1968 I began to judge dog shows. My worldwide judging schedule eventually occupied so much time that I discontinued breeding and showing dogs.

This proved to be no problem until several years later when I met my first bichon frise. At that time bichons were very rare in America and not yet recognized by the American Kennel Club. I was to learn the proper pronunciation of the breed's name: bee-*shawn* free-*say* (plural, bee-*shawns* free-*says*). I was enchanted by this little breed and soon owned one, then two. Eventually I was involved in a full-scale breeding program that produced many famous champions.

Many of these champions were also personal companions and each had its own charm and personality. Most of the bichons I bred went to private homes where they lived to amazingly advanced ages as loved and loving members of their respective households.

The bichon frise has a zest for life and is willing and able to hike, retrieve a ball, or roughhouse for hours. Yet this same bichon is just as content to sit by your side while you read, listen to music, or watch your favorite television program.

As you read *The Bichon Frise: A Complete Pet Owner's Manual,* you will realize how much a "people dog" the bichon has been through the centuries. You will see how totally unsuited this breed is to an isolated life in a kennel. The more time the bichon spends with humans, the more fully its personality develops.

A bichon can be an ideal companion for both young and old and can be equally happy in a small apartment or country estate. This adaptability does not mean it is a breed that requires little or no care—not so! To keep a bichon in good health and looking smart, its white, soft, curly coat requires regular bathing and grooming. If properly taken care of, the bichon rewards its owner with many years of companionship and entertainment.

It is my sincere desire that the following pages will give the reader an introduction to one of the canine world's most charming members. If the reader has already met or is captivated by one of these beguiling companions, it is my fondest wish that what is contained in *The Bichon Frise: A Complete Pet Owner's Manual* will lead to an even more satisfying relationship.

Richard G. Beauchamp

Acknowledgment

The author wishes to acknowledge professional handlers Joe and Pauline Waterman and bichon breeders Gene and Mary Ellen Mills from whom I learned so much about the proper care of bichons frises. Without their knowledge and dedication it would not have been possible to write this book.

The Bichon Frise: Where It Came From; What It Is Today

As difficult as it may be to conceive, the diminutive and delicate looking Italian greyhound, the stalwart bulldog, and the massive Great Dane all trace back to a common ancestor. That ancestor is none other than the one we know today as *Canis lupus*—the wolf.

The wolf's transition from antagonist to "man's best friend" began somewhere in the Mesolithic period, which was over ten thousand years ago. Just providing food for self and family and staying out of harm's way was undoubtedly the Mesolithic human's major concern in life. This in itself was no mean feat considering that use of tools was extremely limited at this stage of human development. Observation of the wolf might have taught some effective hunting techniques. Many of the wolf's social habits might have seemed strikingly familiar. The association grew from there.

As the relationship developed through the ages, certain descendants of these increasingly domesticated wolves could be advantageously selected to assist in hunting and other survival pursuits. The wolves that could assist in satisfying the unending human need for food were of course most highly prized.

Also valued were those wolves that made some kind of warning sound when a marauding neighbor or beast of prey threatened the settlement. The wolves that performed any function that lightened early human existence were cherished and allowed to breed, while those that were not helpful or whose temperament proved incompatible were driven away.

With the passing of time humans realized they could manipulate breedings of these *wolves-cum-dogs* so that the resulting offspring were extremely proficient in particular areas. While human populations developed a more sophisticated lifestyle, they also thought up new ways in which these domesticated wolves could be of assistance. Customizing the evolving wolves to suit growing human needs was the next step. They became hunting wolves, guard wolves, and herding wolves. The list of useful duties grew and grew.

Romans Classify the Breeds

One can find documentation of controlled breeding practices by Roman writers as early as the first century A.D. The Romans had actually broken down the various types of dogs into six general classifications very similar to the "variety groups" used as a classification method by the American Kennel Club today. Two thousand years ago Roman writers talked of "house guardian dogs, shepherd dogs, sporting dogs, war dogs, scent dogs, and sight dogs."

Many of our modern breeds can trace their ancestry directly to members of these early groups. Other breeds were developed by combining two or more individuals from these different categories to create yet another breed.

One of these combinations was to create a family of dogs known as the "barbichons," later shortened to "bichon." This new family was developed with the use of a medium to large size water-dog called the barbet and a simultaneously existing family of generally white, small "lap" or ladies' dogs that existed in the Mediterranean area as far back as 600–300 B.C. Several breeds of dogs are known to have descended from this origin, including the poodle, the Maltese, and four "varieties" or subgroups of the bichon.

Because most wolves and wild dogs were rather large and dark in color, small, light-colored dogs were intriguing and admired. The small dogs became very popular and soon became members of the immediate household.

Often these companion dogs traveled with their owners. As trading flourished, the little pet dogs from home could be bartered for something else wanted or needed.

The little "bichons" that had eventually evolved accompanied their owners to different parts of the world and were left there as trade for other goods. The dogs soon became established and flourished, developing into four distinct varieties: the bichon Maltaise, the bichon Bolognaise, the bichon Havanese and the bichon Teneriffe. The bichon Teneriffe was to become today's bichon frise.

The Four Bichon Varieties

No one is positive about what other canine mixtures may have been involved at the various places to which these four varieties of bichon immigrated. There does seem agreement that the first of the group, the bichon Maltaise, flourished on the isle of Malta.

Whether this breed is the ancestor of today's Maltese remains controversial. Those who do subscribe to this theory offer as proof the recurring and highly undesirable woolly coat that some Maltese have. The Maltese coat must be straight and silky with no undercoat whatsoever.

Another branch of the family, the Bolognaise, became popular around the Italian city of Bologna. They could often be seen accompanying members of the royal family and members of the court. History records that these bichons were often sent as gifts to members of the French and Spanish royal households as well.

There is scant anatomical difference between today's bichon Bolognaise and the bichon frise (nee Teneriffe). Primarily, the temperament of the Bolognaise is less outgoing than its cousin, and the Bolognaise is presented in the show ring with scissoring done only around the eyes and feet.

There were other migrations of these little dogs that began in the eastern Mediterranean and disembarked in Spain. They eventually found their way along the trade routes to Cuba. It appears the Spanish sailors took the little dogs with them and the ones remaining in Cuba are credited as the forebears of the bichon variety known as the Havanese.

The Havanese is the smaller member of the bichon family—normally around 8 to 11 inches (20–28 cm) at the shoulder. It is shorter in leg, longer in body, and comes in a wide variety of colors.

It seems highly probable that these same Spanish sailors took other members of the bichon family with them in their trading expeditions to the Canary Islands and Teneriffe. How long these bichons remained there and what other blood entered this gene pool is unknown, but the bichon seems to have flourished in the Canary Islands and Teneriffe as well. Eventually their descendants made their way full circle,

Ride 'em cowgirl! Here a champion Bichon illustrates the willingness of the bichon frise to act as comic and performer. Historically the bichon frise has been an important part of circuses and fairs throughout Europe.

not only back to Spain but to Italy as well. This variety of bichon was known as the bichon Teneriffe and the breed was to carry that name for many years.

The Bichon Frise Gets Its Name

So then, when and where did our little white dog we now know as the bichon frise actually come from? There are conflicting answers, but we do know that *The Encyclopedia of Dogs (Thomas Y. Crowell Co., New York),* which was produced with the cooperation and direction of The

Federation Cynologique Internationale, gives the bichon frise's country of origin as France. The Federacion Cynologique Internationale (F.C.I.) is the august organization that presides over all of Europe's canine activities, so if anyone has the answers on European dogs it should be the F.C.I.

History substantiates a series of French invasions of Italy that lasted through most of the 1500s. During that time the French came under the Renaissance influence and adopted Italian culture. Part of the adoption process included the bichon Teneriffe, which then made its appearance in France under Francis I, the patron of the Renaissance, who reigned from 1515 to 1547.

From that point it seems the breed went undercover for a time but was to emerge again briefly as a favorite of the court during the reign of Napoleon III in the early 1800s. By the end of that same century, however, the popularity of the darling of the courtesans diminished again. The bichon Teneriffe became the common dog running the streets, but the breed's agility and ability to learn quickly was to provide a new direction and preserve the breed from extinction.

Even then it was not the least unusual to find the bichon that could jump many times its own height, walk on its hind legs for long distances, and do somersaults. These same capabilities exist in many strains of the breed today.

Organ grinders and peddlers were quick to put the bichon's crowd-pleasing antics to use, soon the little dogs began performing tricks on street corners and in the circuses and fairs throughout France. The little bichons clowned about, pawed the air as though they were begging for money and applause, and their owners reaped the monetary rewards. The breed's characteristic of pawing the air was of course highly prized by the organ grinders and evidently selected for inbreeding programs, as it has become an established trait of the breed.

World War I nearly cost the bichon its life as a breed, but for its incredible hardiness and will to survive. Soldiers of many countries, enchanted by the sturdy and clever white charmers, departed for home with bichons as pets. But none of these isolated specimens appears to have been used to initiate a breeding program.

Finally, with decimated stock somewhat replenished by interested breeders after World War I, the first official standard of excellence was written for the bichon frise in France, and that standard was adopted by the Société Centrale Canine in March, 1933. This standard gave the breed its first official and far more descriptive name, "the bichon a poil frise" (the bichon of the curly hair).

With the advent of World War II, the bichon had to withstand yet another devastating blow to its numbers in Europe. Again the breed's tenacity prevailed and the bichon somehow managed to survive. Fortunately, the early 1950's were to prove a turning point for the breed when it embarked upon a journey to America.

The Bichon Comes to America

Helene and Francois Picault of Dieppe, France, became interested in the bichon and began to breed and also show their dogs at various all-breed events. The Picaults migrated to Milwaukee, Wisconsin in 1952, bringing with them their rapidly growing family of bichons in hopes of popularizing and selling the breed in the United States.

Unfortunately their enthusiasm and hopes for the breed in America met with little success. Neither did the Picaults appreciate Milwaukee's frigid

European circus owners and organ grinders in the 1800s were first to discover the bichon's ability to stand on its hind legs and beg with its paws. This delighted spectators then and it continues to do so now as the breed has retained this ability down through many generations.

winters. They decided to move and shortly thereafter took dogs and all to southern California, where they came in contact with collie breeder, Gertrude Fournier. Mrs. Fournier became enchanted with the breed and struggled valiantly to achieve popularity for the bichon in the United States, but it was not until she enlisted the interest and support of Barbara Stubbs of La Jolla, California, that a successful plan was initiated and followed. A club devoted to promoting the best interests of the breed was organized under the name Bichon Frise Club of America, and serious efforts began to make the breed better known.

The Breed Catches On

In the late 1960s, with the promotional assistance of *Kennel Review* magazine, the breed caught the attention of the dog show exhibitors. Within just a few years the bichon skyrocketed to popularity with those who were breeding and showing dogs under American Kennel Club jurisdiction.

In April of 1973 the bichon frise was recognized by the American Kennel Club and admitted to compete for championship points as a member of the Nonsporting Group classification. In July of that same year the first all-breed Best In Show to be won by a bichon took place at Framington Valley Kennel Club. The dog was Mrs. William Tabler's Champion Chaminade Syncopation, which was bred by Barbara Stubbs and Richard Beauchamp. Many more Best-In-Show awards were to follow for Syncopation and others of the breed. International popularity came rapidly for this breed that was doing so well in the United States, and many American-bred bichons were exported to all parts of the world.

In 1985 a bichon frise female, Champion Devon Puff and Stuff, bred and owned by Nancy Shapland, was not only the top winner in her breed but the top winner in the Nonsporting Group as well. Puff was a ringside favorite because of her antics in the show ring, often escaping from her handler and leading him on a merry chase.

One of these escapades was captured on national television when Puff was competing in the Nonsporting Group at Westminster Kennel Club at Madison Square Garden in New York. That night the little extrovert was finally captured by her handler, while Puff herself captured the number one spot in the finals. Puff's clowning endeared her to the television audience all over America, making the name bichon frise synonymous with everything spontaneous and fun-loving in a canine companion. Since then the bichon has continued to grow in favor with the general public, with registrations steadily increasing with each passing year.

The American Kennel Club Breed Standard

The American Kennel Club, which is the chief registering agency for pure-bred dogs in America, provides a standard of excellence for every breed that it recognizes. The standard stipulates all characteristics that an ideal specimen of the breed should have.

It must be remembered that no dog is perfect and none adhere entirely to a given breed standard. The standard is used as a guideline by the breeder and as a blueprint by the dog judge to evaluate all entries.

The following is a summary of the most important characteristics the official standard of excellence lists for the bichon frise. A complete copy of the official breed standard along with additional informative literature may be obtained by writing to the Bichon Frise Club of America. The address of the club appears at the end of this book in the section entitled *Useful Addresses and Literature.*

General appearance: The bichon frise is a small, sturdy, white powder puff of a dog whose merry temperament is evidenced by a plumed tail carried jauntily over the back and a dark-eyed inquisitive expression.

Size, proportion, substance: The adult bichon frise should measure between 9½ inches (24.36 cm) and 11½ inches (29.4 cm) at the shoulder. (The minimum heights do not apply to puppies.) The height requirement is the same for both males and females but usually the female is slightly smaller than the male. The bichon is a compact dog: the length of body from chest to buttocks is only slightly greater than the measure of the dog from the highest point of the shoulder to the ground. The breed is neither coarse and heavy of bone nor is it fragile or fine.

Head and expression: The bichon's dark-eyed, inquisitive, and alert expression is more than anything else the essence of the breed's appeal. The eyes should be large and dark brown or black. Eyes of any other color or those that are either bulging or small and squinty are completely incorrect. Surrounding the bichon's eyes there is black or very dark brown pigment, referred to as halos. These are necessary, as they accentuate the eye and enhance the expression. The eye rims themselves should be black. The ears hang loosely on the sides of the head just above eye level. The skull itself is slightly rounded, and the juncture between the muzzle and the head (called the stop) is slightly accentuated. The length of the muzzle is slightly shorter than the length of the skull as 3 is to 5. Looking down at the head from above, a line drawn between the outside corners of the eyes and the end of the nose would constitute a near-equilateral triangle. The nose is prominent and always black. The lips are black as well and are never pendulous or drooping. The bichon has what is referred to as a scissors bite, that is, the outer surfaces of the lower incisors touch the inner surfaces of the upper incisors. Overshot or undershot bites are serious faults, as are missing teeth.

Neck, topline, and body: The neck is long and carried proudly behind an erect head. The length of the neck is

This picture portrays a quality bichon frise as described in the American Kennel Club breed standard.

The beautiful toy poodle; this dog shows how different the breed is from the bichon frise.

This is an outstanding representative of the Maltese breed and illustrates how the breed differs from the bichon frise.

approximately one third of the distance from forechest to buttocks. The topline is level except for a slight muscular rise over the loin area. The chest is well developed and wide enough to allow free and unrestricted movement of the front legs. The lowest point of the chest should reach the elbow. The ribs are well sprung and the forechest is well pronounced. The tail is well plumed, set on level with the topline and carried curved gracefully over the back so that the hair of the tail rests on the back. Tails carried perpendicularly to the back or those that droop behind are serious faults. A corkscrew tail is a very serious fault.

Forequarters: The shoulder blade, upper arm, and forearm are approximately equal in length. The shoulder itself is laid back to somewhat near a forty-five degree angle. When viewed from the side, the upper arm extends back so that the elbow is placed directly below the withers. Legs are of

medium bone. They are straight with no curve or bow in the forearm or wrist. The elbows are held close to the body. The pasterns slope slightly from the vertical. Dewclaws may be

A champion bichon in one of the many important wins acquired while attaining the title of "Top Winning Bichon Frise of All Time." Her show ring antics made her a crowd favorite everywhere she was shown.

13

How the Bichon Differs from the Maltese and the Poodle

As we have noted in the bichon frise's early history, the breed descended from the same rootstock that produced not only the other varieties of bichon, but the Maltese and the poodle as well. Be clear that the bichon frise is not the result of a cross between the Maltese and the toy poodle. Our bichon frise is a descendant of the same rootstock that produced the other two breeds. In other words, the three are "cousins," all tracing back to the same ancestors. As the three breeds journeyed along from their earliest origins, definite breed characteristics evolved. The distinguishing major differences are as follows:

Maltese

Coat: the Maltese coat is "single;" that is without any woolly undercoat. It hangs long, flat, and silky over the sides of the body, most often to the ground. The hair may not be kinky, curly, or woolly. There is no shaving and little scissoring of the coat.

Color: pure white; light tan, or lemon on ears is permissible but not desirable.

Size: weight under seven pounds with four to six pounds preferred. No specification is given for height.

Toy Poodle

Coat: curly, of a naturally harsh texture, dense throughout. Presented at dog shows in standard prescribed clips, usually with the face, base of tail, and feet shaved and the remainder clipped to a specific pattern.

Color: solid colors only to include blues, grays, silvers, browns, cafe-au-laits, apricot, and cream, which are in reality only dilutions of black, white, and brown.

Size: weight is not considered; requirement is that it is ten inches tall (25.6 cm) or less, measured at the highest point of shoulder.

Bichon Frise

Coat: undercoat is soft and dense, the outercoat of a coarser and curlier texture. The combination of the two feels soft but substantial. When bathed and brushed, the coat stands off the body like a powder puff. The coat is trimmed to reveal the natural outline of the body.

Color: color is white, but there may be shadings of buff, cream, or apricot around the ears and on the body. No off-white color in excess of ten percent of the entire coat is allowed on a mature specimen.

Size: 9½ to 11½ inches (24.36–29.4 cm) measured at the shoulder is considered the ideal size range; no weight requirements given.

removed. The feet, which are tight, round, and point directly forward, resemble those of a cat. The feet point neither in nor out. The foot pads are black and the nails are kept short.

Hindquarters: The hindquarters are of medium bone, well muscled and well angulated. They are spaced moderately wide. The upper and lower thighs are nearly equal in length, meeting in a well-bent stifle joint. The

leg from hock joint to foot pad is perpendicular to the ground. Dewclaws may be removed. The paws are tight and round with black pads.

Coat: The bichon's coat is one of its most distinctive features and texture is of utmost importance. The undercoat is soft and dense, while the outercoat is of a coarser and curlier texture. The combination of the two feels soft but substantial, like plush or velvet. When patted, the coat springs back into place. When bathed and brushed, the coat stands off the body, creating an overall powder puff appearance. Wiry coats are not desirable, nor are limp, silky coats. Lack of undercoat is a serious fault in the adult bichon. The coat is trimmed to reveal the natural outline of the body. It is rounded off from any direction and never cut so short as to create an overly trimmed or squared-off appearance. The furnishings of the head, beard, mustache, ears, and tail are left longer. The longer head hair is trimmed to create an overall rounded impression. The topline is trimmed to appear level. The coat is long enough to maintain the powder puff look that is characteristic of the breed.

Color: The coat color is white, but some shading of buff, cream, or apricot around the ears or on the body is permissible. Any color other than white in excess of ten percent of the entire coat of a mature specimen is a fault. Color of the accepted shadings is not to be faulted in puppies.

Gait: Movement at a trot is free, precise, and effortless. In profile the forelegs and hind legs extend equally with an easy reach and drive. When moving, the topline remains steady and the head and neck are held somewhat erect. There is a slight convergence of the legs toward the center line as speed increases. Moving away, the hindquarters travel with moderate width between them and the foot pads can easily be seen. The movement is true and precise both coming and going.

Temperament: The bichon is gentle-mannered, sensitive, playful, and affectionate. A cheerful attitude is the hallmark of the breed and nothing less should be acceptable.

Choosing Your Bichon: Your Needs; Its Needs

There are few subjects for the photographer's art that have greater appeal than a litter of puppies snuggled together and fast asleep in a wicker basket or gift box. We see these enticing pictures on greeting cards and calendars everywhere. Many times this is what will inspire well-meaning individuals to rush out and buy a puppy for themselves or as a gift for a loved one. All puppies are cuddly and cute and may even spend a part of their day duplicating those appealing greeting card and calendar poses. It is important to realize though that a puppy will spend only a very small part of its day doing so. The far greater part of the day and night the puppy will spend investigating, digging, chewing, eating, relieving itself, needing to go outdoors and then immediately insisting that it be let in. All too often these needs are not considered realistically before adding a dog to one's household.

The list of the real needs of a young puppy or an adult dog can be staggering to the uninitiated, and it takes a very concerned and dedicated human being to fulfill these needs. This is to say nothing of the time required for the many lessons a dog must be taught by its master before it understands what it may and may not do.

Friends often seek our advice when they are contemplating the purchase of their first dog. If we detect even the slightest uncertainty on their part, we always advise them to wait until they are absolutely sure they want to take

on this great responsibility. Owning a dog takes a great commitment and it is not something that should ever be done on a whim. The hasty purchase of a dog can result in sheer drudgery and frustration for the owner and an unhappy situation for the dog itself.

Failure to understand the amount of time and consideration a well-cared-for dog requires is one of the primary reasons for the many unwanted canines that end their lives in an animal shelter. Given proper consideration beforehand, the purchase of a dog can bring a person many years of companionship and comfort as well as unconditional devotion no other animal can match.

In addition to these three major questions regarding dog ownership, it behooves the prospective dog owner to strongly consider the specific peculiarities of his or her own life-style or household. All this applies whether the household is made up of a single individual or a large family. Everyone involved must realize the new dog will not understand the household routine and must be taught *everything* you want it to know and do. This takes time and patience, and very often the most important lessons for the new dog to learn will take the longest for it to absorb.

Why a Purebred Dog?

There is no difference in the love, devotion, and companionship that a mixed-breed dog and a purebred dog can give its owner. There are, however, some aspects of suitability that

What could be more appealing than a basketful of cuddly bichon frise puppies?

Should You Own a Dog?

Three very important questions:

1. Does the person who will ultimately be responsible for the dog's day-to-day care really want a dog?

In many active families the mother of the household is the person who will have the ultimate responsibility for the family dog. She may not want any more duties than she already has. Pet care can be an excellent way to teach children responsibility, but beware—in their enthusiasm to have a puppy, children are apt to promise almost anything. It is what will happen after the novelty of a new dog has worn off that must be looked at.

2. Does the life-style and schedule of the household lend itself to the demands of proper dog care?

This means there must always be someone available to see to the dog's basic needs: feeding, exercise, coat care, access to the outdoors when required, and the like.

3. Is the kind of dog being considered suitable for the individual or household?

Very young children can unknowingly be very rough and unintentionally hurt a young puppy of a small breed. On the other hand, a young dog of a very large breed can overwhelm and sometimes injure an infant or small child in an overly enthusiastic moment. Sharing a tiny apartment with a giant breed can prove extremely difficult for both dog and owner. Toy breeds will have difficulty surviving northern winters if required to live outdoors in unheated quarters. A long-haired dog, while attractive, is hardly suitable for the individual who spends most outdoor time camping, hunting, or hiking through the woods.

can best be fulfilled by the purebred dog.

All puppies, purebred or not, are cute, but it stands to reason not all puppies will grow up to be particularly attractive adults. It is nearly impossible to predict what a mixed-breed puppy will look like at maturity. Size, length of hair, and temperament can vary widely and may not be at all what the owner had hoped for. What then happens to the dog?

In buying a purebred puppy the purchaser will have a very good idea of what the dog will look like and how it will behave as an adult. Purebred dogs have been bred for generations to meet specifications of conformation and temperament.

When choosing a puppy one must have the adult dog in mind, because the adult dog should fit the owner's life-style and esthetic standards. A very fastidious housekeeper may have trouble accommodating a large breed that sheds its coat the year round. Joggers or long-distance runners who want a dog to accompany them are not going to be happy with a short-legged or slow breed. It is also important to know that short-muzzled dogs and those with "pushed-in" faces have very little heat tolerance. These are the things that must be considered *before* you select a puppy.

Since the conformation of purebred dogs is entirely predictable, the owner of a purebred puppy will know that the breed selected will still be appropriate as an adult. Temperament in purebred dogs has great predictability, although it might have minor variations within a breed. The hair-trigger response and hyperactivity of certain breeds would not be at all suitable for someone who wants a quiet, contented companion, nor would the placid attitude of yet other breeds be desirable for someone who wants an athletic, exuberant dog to frolic with. With purebred dogs, you

are reasonably assured of selecting a dog compatible with your life-style.

The purchase price of a purebred dog will be a significant investment for the owner, but a purebred dog costs no more to maintain than a mixed breed. If the cost of having exactly the kind of dog you want and are proud to own is gauged over the number of years you will enjoy it, you will have to admit the initial cost becomes less consequential.

Before hastily buying a breed of dog whose *appearance* you find appealing, spend time with adult members of the breed or do some good research to assure yourself that you and the breed in question are temperamentally compatible. Many books have been written about the various breeds and often devote a good amount of space discussing the temperament of the breed and its compatibility. Visiting kennels or breeders specializing in the breed of your choice will assist you enormously in deciding if you are considering the right breed for you.

Is the Bichon Frise the Right Dog for Me?

The entire history of the bichon frise has been one of constant and close association with people. The bichon has been the sailor's companion, favorite of royal families, a circus performer, and war refugee.

I think this incredible versatility and hardiness makes the bichon frise one of the most adaptable of all breeds. The bichon is suitable for an amazingly wide variety of living situations. First, the breed is a very good size—not too large for even the smallest apartment, nor on the other hand so small as to be at risk in a household of growing children.

The American Kennel Club standard of the breed states the size of the bichon frise should fall somewhere within the limits of 9½ and 11½ inches (24.36–29.4 cm) when measured at the shoulder. The average size for the breed is probably around 10½ inches (27 cm). Some individuals, of course, grow up to be smaller and others will be larger than average, but experienced breeders are able to predict roughly at which end of the size spectrum an individual bichon puppy will mature.

Of the many breeds that we have owned and bred we can honestly say the bichon is one of the most amiable. The breed can be equally at home with children and with the elderly. It is easily compatible with breeds much larger than itself as well as the tiniest of toy breeds. Introduced early enough, even cats can be a bichon's friend and companion.

We know of households that keep several full-grown male bichons together. While this can be a volatile situation in many breeds, there is seldom the least aggressive behavior by any of them. Bichons seem easily and happily able to adjust themselves to the needs of whomever they live with.

The bichon frise in full show trim may look fragile and delicate to some, but that look is entirely deceiving. Under the well-groomed coat is a sturdy, agile, and sound little dog that is constructed to be able to keep up easily with the most active youngster or adult. One must not forget the "street dog" heritage of the bichon. This is a breed that historically has had to handle itself in all kinds of situations. Always ready for a good romp, a long hike, or a jog in the park, the bichon is not hyperactive and overly excitable and is equally content to spend a quiet afternoon or evening with an owner who is in a contemplative mood.

The bichon is a built-in alarm system. The breed is very protective of its home and territory and will sound the alarm when necessary, yet is not prone to excessive barking.

A much appreciated attribute of this breed is its practically odor-free and nonshedding coat. That in itself is a major consideration for a lot of people who object to a lifetime of sweeping, vacuuming the house, and brushing hair off clothing.

Other Considerations

As adaptable and amiable a breed as the bichon frise is, there are other criteria to be weighed. The freshly bathed and groomed bichon certainly presents an attractive picture, but as exhibitors and breeders are inclined to say, "They look that way for about five minutes." The bichon appears to be the eternal child and loves playing in the mud and digging holes as much as any human youngster. This can wreak havoc on that white, curly coat, and a bichon seems to find the best time for a romp in the mud is right after a bath. While the bichon coat does not shed, it does mat and tangle and requires regular bathing, trimming, and grooming to maintain that jaunty, tailored look that is a good part of its attraction. The pet owner should plan on devoting at least 20 to 30 minutes twice a week to keeping the bichon tangle free.

Digging in the garden has great appeal for the bichon, especially after a bath!

The bichon frise seems to fit in almost anywhere and are happy just so long as their human friends are nearby.

The breed's need of trimming will require either learning to do it properly yourself or employing the services of a professional groomer. We have included the section "Bathing and Grooming" for those who wish to become proficient in this area. With time, practice, and the right grooming tools, the art can be mastered.

Some good professionals charge a hefty fee for their services, but those owners who insist their bichon maintain the very special look of the breed find the results well worth the charge. Bichon owners must either be prepared to put in a fair amount of work

on their dog each week or budget the funds to have a professional do the work. Professional groomers charge about $35 to $50 for a bath and pet-type trim and about $75 to prepare a bichon for the show ring.

While the bichon appears to be generally nonallergic to humans, like many white, pink-skinned dogs, it can be extremely flea sensitive. If ignored, this sensitivity can lead to severe scratching, skin eruptions, and "hot spots" accompanied by hair loss.

Careful owners can, however, avoid these problems by constant surveillance and prevention. There are many

Some owners call the bichon frise "the dog you can take anywhere" in that the breed is as happy taking a romp in the park as it is spending a quiet evening at home watching TV.

commercial flea-exterminating services that will come to your home periodically and spray the premises, both indoor and out, thus assuring you of keeping the problem in abeyance.

Male or Female?

While some individuals may have their personal preferences for the sex of their dog, we can honestly say that both the male and the female bichon frise are equal in their trainability and affection. The decision will have more to do with the life-style and ultimate plans of the owner than differences between the sexes in the breed.

There is one point the prospective buyer should consider. While both the male and the female bichon must be trained not to urinate in the home, the male does provide an additional problem. The male of any breed of dog has a natural instinct to lift his leg and urinate on objects to establish and "mark" his territory. The degree of effort that must be invested in training the male not to do this varies with the individual dog. This habit becomes increasingly more difficult to correct with the number of times a male dog is used for breeding. The mating act increases his need and desire to mark his territory.

On the other hand, one must realize that the female will have her semiannual and sometimes burdensome heat cycle after she is eight or nine months old. At these times she must be confined to avoid soiling her surroundings, and she must also be closely watched to prevent male dogs gaining access to her or she will become pregnant.

Both of these sexually associated problems can be eliminated by having the pet bichon "altered." Spaying the female and neutering the male will not change the character of your pet and will avoid the problems involved were you to choose not to do so. Neutering also precludes the possibility of your pet adding to the extreme pet overpopulation problem that concerns environmentalists worldwide.

It is important to understand though that these are not reversible procedures. If you are considering the possibility of showing your bichon, altered animals are not allowed to compete in American Kennel Club conformation dog shows. Altered animals may however compete in obedience trials, agility events, and field trials.

Where to Buy Your Bichon

Your bichon will live with you many years. This is a breed that regularly lives to be ten, twelve, and often fourteen years of age. It is extremely important therefore that it comes from a source where physical and mental soundness are primary considerations in the breeding program. This is usually the result of careful breeding over a period of many years. Selective breeding is aimed at maintaining the virtues of the breed and eliminating genetic weaknesses. Because this selective breeding is time-consuming and costly, good breeders protect their investment by providing the best prenatal care for their breeding females and nutrition for the growing puppies. There is no substitute for the amount of dedication and care good breeders give their dogs.

The Bichon Frise Club of America and the American Kennel Club can both provide the prospective buyer with the names and addresses of responsible individuals who have intelligently bred bichons available for sale. Many local pet stores will carry a list of good breeders and can refer you directly to them as well.

A pet shop should be able to provide the same information about a puppy's background that you would get directly from a breeder, such as the pedigrees and health records of the puppy's parents; whether the puppy was raised around people or in a cage; how long it stayed with the mother; and so forth. The store should also guarantee that it will take back the puppy if it becomes ill.

There is a good chance that there are reputable breeders located nearby who will not only be able to provide the bichon you are looking for but who will be able to advise you regularly in proper care and feeding. These breeders normally have on the premises the parents and other relatives of the bichon you are interested in. The majority of these breeders will be more than happy to have you see their dogs and to discuss the advantages and responsibilities involved in owning the breed. Responsible breeders are as concerned about their stock being placed in the right hands as you, the prospective buyer, are in having a sound and healthy dog.

Do not hesitate to ask questions and to ask to see the breeder's mature dogs. Experienced breeders know which hereditary problems exist in bichons and will be happy to discuss them with you. Practically all breeds are subject to inherited ailments, and bichons are no exception.

Helpful hint: Beware of breeders who tell you that their dogs are not susceptible to inherited diseases or

A family portrait. Hobby breeders provide some of the best purebred dogs offered for sale. This photograph represents three generations of bichon frises.

potential problems. I do not mean to imply that all bichons are afflicted with genetic problems, but a reliable breeder will give you the information you are entitled to regarding the individual bichon you are considering. The chapter "Inherited Problems and Diseases" will give details on some of the genetic ailments that might exist.

Temperament and health of the parents of your prospective purchase are of paramount importance. If you dislike what you observe in either of the parents, *look elsewhere!*

Inspect the environment in which the dogs are raised. Cleanliness is as important to producing good stock as are good pedigrees. The time you spend in researching and inspecting the kennel and the adult dogs it houses may well save you a great deal of money and heartache in the years to come.

All this is not to imply your bichon puppy must come from a large kennel. On the contrary, many good puppies are produced by small hobby breeders in their homes. These names may well be included in recommendations from both the American Kennel Club and the Bichon Frise Club of America. These individuals offer the same investment of time, study, and knowledge as the larger kennel and they are just as ready to offer the same health guarantees.

A newspaper advertisement may or may not lead you to a reputable hobby breeder. It is up to you to investigate and compare as you would in the case of any major purchase. Good hobby breeders will sell only to approved buyers and spend considerable time in determining this. If the seller is willing to let you make a purchase with no questions asked, you should be highly suspicious.

Conformation and sound structure are very important in the bichon frise breed. Even a young puppy should appear sound and sturdy.

Selecting a Bichon Puppy

The bichon you want to buy should be a happy, playful extrovert. Never select a puppy that appears frail or sickly because you feel sorry for it. Bichon puppies with positive temperaments are not afraid of strangers. Under normal circumstances you will have the whole litter in your lap if you kneel and call them to you. Avoid the puppy that cowers in a corner and tries to run away from you.

If one puppy in particular appeals to you, pick it up and, if possible, carry it off to an area nearby where the two of you can spend some time alone. As long as a puppy is still in a fairly familiar environment where scents and sounds are not entirely strange, it should retain its outgoing personality.

Helpful hint: When you and your prospective puppy are alone, you will have an opportunity to examine the puppy more closely. Check the puppy's ears. They should be pink and clean. Any odor or dark discharge could indicate ear mites, which in turn would indicate poor maintenance. The inside of the mouth and gums should also be pink, and the teeth should be clean and white. There should be no malformation of the mouth or jaw. The dark eyes should be clear and bright. Again, be aware of any signs of discharge.

As small as bichon puppies are, they should feel compact and substantial to the touch, never bony and undernourished; neither should they be bloated. A taut and bloated abdomen is usually a sign of worms.

However, a rounded puppy belly is normal. The nose of a bichon puppy should not be crusted or running. A cough or diarrhea is a danger signal as are any kinds of eruptions on the skin.

Conformation is important even at an early age. The bichon puppy's legs should be straight. As the pup walks toward you its front legs should move directly forward, as should the rear legs when the pup is moving away from you. The movement should be free and easy.

The show prospect puppy must be sound and healthy and must also show promise that it will conform closely to the AKC standard of the breed at maturity. Pictured is a Champion Bichon when she was just eight weeks of age.

Veterinary Health Check

Most breeders are more than happy to supply a written agreement that the sale of a puppy is contingent upon the puppy's successfully passing a veterinary health check. If the locations of the breeder, your home, and your prospective veterinarian allow it, plan the time of day you pick up your puppy so that you can go directly from the breeder to the veterinarian. If this is not possible, you should plan the visit as soon as possible. No longer than 24 hours should elapse before this is done. Should the puppy not pass the veterinary health check, a responsible breeder will be more than happy either to refund your money or provide you with another puppy.

If you have been reading and doing your research you can expect the bichon puppy to look almost like a miniaturized version of an adult, aside from the length and texture of coat. Bichon puppies have very soft coats, nothing like the firm, "powder puff" texture required for adults.

Best Age for Selection

Raising a puppy is a wonderful experience. Granted, at times it can also be one of the most exasperating experiences you have ever attempted. In the end though, having endured each other through all the trials of puppyhood, you and your bichon will forge a bond that has no equal.

Should you decide you do in fact wish to raise this bit of fluff from infancy to adulthood, be aware that most breeders do not and should not release their puppies until they have had their initial inoculations, which is about eight to ten weeks of age. Do not remove a puppy from its home environment before it has been vaccinated.

Prior to immunization, puppies are very susceptible to infectious diseases. Many such diseases may be transmitted via the clothing and hands of people. After the first series of vaccinations the breeder will inform you when your bichon puppy is ready to leave its first home.

Show Dog or Companion?

If dog shows and breeding are in the future of your bichon puppy, the older it is at time of selection the more likely you will know how good a dog you will have at maturity. The most any breeder can say about an eight-week-old bichon puppy is that it has or does not have "show potential." If you are seriously interested in having a bichon of the quality to show or to breed, wait with your selection until the puppy is at least five to six months old. By this time you can be far more certain of dentition, soundness, and attitude, as well as other important characteristics. No matter what you have in mind for your bichon's future—dog shows or nothing more than loving companionship—all the foregoing should be considered carefully.

If the excitement and pride of owning a winning show dog appeals to you, we can not urge you too strongly to seek out a successful breeder who has a record of having produced winning dogs through the years. As stated, it is extremely difficult, if not impossible, to predict what an eight-week-old puppy will look like as an adult. An experienced breeder, however, will know whether a young puppy has "potential." Unfortunately most prospective owners want both a very young puppy and some guarantee that the puppy will grow up to be a winning show dog. It is not possible to give that kind of guarantee, and no honest breeder will do so.

Show-Prospect Puppies

A show-prospect puppy must not only adhere to all the health and soundness qualifications of the good pet puppy, it must show every sign that it will conform very closely to the rigid demands of the breed standard when it matures. It might make little difference to you if your pet is a bit longer in body or shorter on leg than what the breed standard considers ideal, but faults like this make considerable difference in determining the future of a show dog.

All male show dogs must have two normal-sized testicles in the scrotum. Some males only have one testicle and this eliminates them from being considered as a show prospect. Certainly this would make no difference to pet owners who will have their male dog sexually altered anyway. Therefore purchasing a male with this "fault" could give the buyer a beautiful dog not otherwise affordable.

Your chances of obtaining a bichon puppy that will mature into a winning adult are far better if purchased from a breeder whose bichon bloodline has produced many champions. Even at that, no one can be sure of having a winner until the puppy has reached maturity. Obviously a puppy six or seven months old or a young adult will provide much more certainty.

We have known some people who have spent thousands of dollars buying very young bichon puppies again and again but have never achieved their goal of owning a winning show dog. Granted, an older puppy or grown dog may initially cost considerably more than an eight-week-old puppy, but odds are much greater that in the end you will have what you actually wanted.

Experienced and successful bichon breeders have spent years developing a line of top-quality animals. These breeders know what to look for in the breed and they are particularly familiar with the manner in which their own stock matures. It is important to understand that while a show dog will provide the same amount of love and devotion as one purchased strictly as a pet, you will have a great deal more work in coat care and maintenance.

Price

The price of a bichon puppy can vary considerably, but do understand that reputable breeders have invested considerable time, skill, and work to make sure they have the best possible breeding stock. This costs a great deal of money. Good breeders have also invested substantially in veterinary supervision and testing to keep their stock as free from hereditary defects as possible.

A puppy purchased from an established and successful breeder may cost more initially, but the small additional investment can save many trips to the veterinarian over the ensuing years. It is heartbreaking to become attached to a dog only to lose it an early age because of some health defect.

You should expect to pay $600 or more for an eight-week-old, pet-quality

Established breeders spend a great deal of money developing a line of sound and healthy bichons. While the initial purchase price may reflect this investment, the breeder's care and concern can save the buyer many expensive trips to the veterinarian.

bichon frise puppy. Older puppies will cost more. Youngsters with show and breeding potential may be double that price and young show stock that has reached the five- or six-month-old stage will be again more expensive.

Inoculations and Health Certificates

By twelve weeks of age most puppies have been vaccinated against hepatitis, leptospirosis, distemper, and canine parvovirus. Rabies inoculations are usually not given until the puppy is six months of age. There is a set series of inoculations developed to combat these infectious diseases and more details are given in the chapter *Veterinary Care.*

You are entitled to have a record of these inoculations when you purchase your bichon. Most breeders will give you complete documentation of this, along with dates on which your puppy was wormed and examined by the

Your bichon's pedigree and registration certificate are important documents the breeder will supply when you purchase your puppy.

Adopting an older bichon can be a delightful experience for both dog and owner. Bringing a mature bichon into the home eliminates all the trials and tribulations of puppyhood.

veterinarian. Usually this record will also indicate when "booster" shots are required. These are very important records to keep; they will be needed by the veterinarian you choose for care of your bichon.

Pedigree and Registration Certificate

Buying a purebred dog also entitles you to a copy of the dog's pedigree and registration certificate. These are two separate documents. The former is simply the dog's family tree. It lists the registered names of your bichon's sire and dam along with their ancestors for several generations.

The registration certificate is issued by the American Kennel Club. When ownership of your bichon is transferred from the breeder's name to your name, the transaction is entered on this certificate, and once mailed to the AKC it is permanently recorded in their computerized records. The AKC will send you a copy of the duly recorded change. File this document in a safe place along with your other important papers, as you will need it should you ever wish to show or breed your bichon.

Diet Sheet

A sound and healthy bichon puppy is in that condition because it has been properly fed and cared for. Every breeder has a slightly different approach to successful nutrition, so it is wise to obtain a written record or description that details the amount and kind of food your puppy has been receiving. It should also indicate the number of times a day your bichon puppy has been accustomed to being fed and the kind of vitamin supplementation it has been receiving. Maintaining this system at least for the first week or two after your puppy comes home with you will reduce the chances of digestive upsets and loose stools. A good diet program also projects increases in food

It is important that puppies have all their initial inoculations before they are taken to their new homes. This is usually at about eight to ten weeks of age.

and changes that should be made in the dog's diet as it matures.

Consider an Adult Bichon

A very young puppy is not your only option for adding a bichon to your household. For some people, especially the elderly, a housebroken adult can be an excellent choice. Also, if time available to housebreak is limited or the owner expects to be away from home frequently, an adult bichon can be a wise choice.

Practically all bichons, even adults, seem to adapt to their new environments very easily. This cannot be said for all other breeds. The mature bichon also needs far less supervision than a puppy, because it has normally passed through the mischievous stage and the need to chew. Usually an adult bichon is ready, willing, and *capable* of learning the household routine.

There are some important things to consider in bringing an adult bichon into your home. The adult dog may have developed habits that you do not find acceptable. In some cases it may

be difficult to retrain such animals. Until you begin to work together, there is no way of knowing how willing an adult bichon is to learn new habits. Always take an adult dog home on a trial basis to see how it works out for both you and the dog.

Another factor to consider is that some adult bichons may never have interacted with little children. If there are young children in your home, the first sight of these "miniature people" can be very perplexing and frightening to the inexperienced bichon. It may take time and patience to overcome initial fears, but with perseverance and good judgment it is usually not too difficult a task. Most bichons I have observed have a natural affinity with children.

Giving the adult bichon not used to small children an area of its own where the children are excluded is vitally important. An adult bichon nearly always comes around and accepts children when it is ready, but if children continually rush up to grab the dog or, worse yet, chase after it, this simply reinforces the fearful behavior.

Care of the Bichon Puppy

Preparing for the New Puppy

There is a great deal you can do prior to your bichon puppy's arrival to make the transition as painless and trauma-free as possible. If possible, visit your puppy several times while it is still in its original home so that you are not entirely a stranger.

Well in advance of the puppy's arrival you can secure the equipment and toys that will be needed and prepare the area in which it will live initially. A fenced-off area in the kitchen is the ideal place to start your puppy off; accidents can be easily cleaned up and the kitchen is a room in which there is

Obtaining the basic equipment before your puppy arrives gives the newcomer a safe little haven of its own. Here the new puppy rests in its crate, enclosed in portable, partitioned fencing. Water bowl, food dish and play toys are easily accessible. The only thing else the puppy needs is your love.

normally a good deal of traffic. Don't forget a young puppy is accustomed to the companionship of its littermates. Without them the puppy will be lonely. It will be up to you to compensate for the loss of your puppy's siblings.

Equipment and Toys

The following is a list of the basic requirements you should already have satisfied when your puppy arrives. The value and use of each will be more fully explained as we proceed.

Partitioned-off living area: Paneled fence partitions about three feet (92 cm) high are available at most major pet shops and are well worth the investment for keeping the puppy where you want it to be. Bichon puppies love to be where their owners are but underfoot is not where a puppy should be.

Cage or shipping kennel: Inside the fenced-off area there should be a wire cage or fiberglass shipping kennel (the open door of which provides access to a sleeping "den"). This cage will also be used for housebreaking. The cage housebreaking method is explained in detail further along in this chapter. These wire cages and fiberglass shipping kennels come in varying sizes. The medium size [approximately 20 inches (51 cm) high by 24 inches (61 cm) wide by 30 inches (77 cm) long] will be the ideal size to accommodate your bichon even as an adult.

Water dish and feeding bowl: These are available made of many different materials. Choose something nonbreakable and not easy to tip over. Bichon puppies very quickly learn to upset the water bowl and relish turning their entire living area into a swimming pool! We recommend plastic or stainless steel bowls that eliminate the worry of toxic content.

Food as recommended on the "diet sheet" obtained from your puppy's breeder: In the unlikely circumstance that you were not provided with this information, there are many highly nutritious commercial brands of dog food available at pet stores and supermarkets that come complete with feeding instructions. Veterinarians are always helpful in this area as well.

Brush and comb: A young bichon's coat does not require a great deal of grooming, but the process should begin early. Equipment that you will need is described in detail in Bathing and Grooming.

Soft collar and a leash: This should be very lightweight and is what you will need to begin initial lead breaking.

Toys: These can be anything you choose, but be sure they are safe—without buttons or strings that can be chewed off or swallowed. Also avoid hard plastic toys that can splinter. Make sure all toys are larger than those that the puppy can get into its mouth. These small toys can become lodged in the mouth and caught in the throat. Do not give your bichon puppy old and discarded shoes or stockings to play with. A puppy is unable to determine the difference between "old" and "new" and unless carefully watched may think it is perfectly all right to add newly acquired dancing slippers to its toy collection.

Bringing Your Puppy Home

The safest way to transport the puppy from kennel to your home is to obtain a pet carrier or cardboard box large enough for the puppy to stretch

out comfortably, with sides high enough so that it can not climb out. Put a layer of newspapers at the bottom in case of accidents and a soft blanket or towel on top of that. Ideally another family member or friend should accompany you to do the driving or hold the carrier that the puppy is in.

Helpful hint: When your puppy arrives at its new home it will be confused and undoubtedly whine in search of its littermates. This will be especially so at night when its littermates are not there to snuggle up to. For the first few nights after the new puppy arrives we put a box next to the bed and let the newcomer sleep there. Should the puppy wake up crying in loneliness, a reassuring hand can be dropped down into the box and we have avoided having to trudge to a different part of the house to quiet the lonely puppy.

Letting the puppy "howl it out" can be a nerve-racking experience that could easily cost you, your family, and your neighbors nights of sleep. Should you wish to transfer the puppy's sleeping quarters to a different part of the house later, you can do this more easily once the puppy has learned to be by itself for increasing periods of time.

Socialization and Safety

It is very important that you accustom the bichon puppy to everyday events as soon as it is practical. Strange noises, children, and other animals can be very frightening when the puppy first encounters them.

Making sure your bichon puppy has enough safe toys of its own will help keep the puppy out of mischief. "Puppy proofing" the area in which the puppy lives is still very important.

Some breeders make it a point to expose their puppies to as many everyday sights and sounds as possible, but this is not always practical when many dogs have to be taken care of. Therefore it is up to you to gently and gradually introduce your puppy to such sounds as the garbage disposal, the vacuum cleaner, and the television set.

Ideally the first time your puppy is exposed to a strange, loud sound you will be able to keep the sound limited to just a few seconds. Once the puppy learns the sound does not present danger, you will be able to increase the length of time. Eventually the puppy will take even the loudest sounds in stride.

We previously mentioned that children can be very frightening to the adult bichon that has never spent time with "little humans." This applies to puppies as well. While many young bichons innately love children, there are exceptions in which puppies with no previous exposure to children are at first frightened by them. Supervising introductions is very important. A quiet, gentle approach on the part of the child normally leads to establishing a lasting friendship, and soon dog and child form a lasting bond.

Regardless of whether the bichon puppy has had prior experience with young children, the children themselves must be educated about what they may and may not do with the new puppy. Learning the gentle approach, exercising caution when the puppy is underfoot, and taking care not to make loud and sudden noises are all lessons that the adult should teach young children as part of responsible dog ownership.

"Puppy Proofing" Your Home

A good part of your bichon puppy's safety depends upon your ability to properly "puppy proof" your home. Electrical outlets, lamp cords, strings, and mouth-size objects of any kind all spell danger to the inquisitive bichon puppy. If you think of your new arrival as one part building inspector and one part vacuum cleaner you will be better equipped to protect your puppy from itself.

Bichon puppies can be ingenious at getting into places they shouldn't be. Things like household cleaning products and gardening supplies should be kept in securely latched cupboards out of a puppy's reach.

There is a product called Bitter Apple that tastes just like it sounds—*terrible!* Actually a furniture cream, it is nonpoisonous and can be used to coat electrical wires and chair legs. In most (not all) cases it will deter your puppy from damaging not only household items but itself as well. Should Bitter Apple not work, there is plastic tubing available at hardware stores which can be put around electrical cords and some furniture legs.

There are baby gates to keep your puppy out and cages and kennels of various kinds to keep your puppy in. All this and a daily "Puppy Proofing Patrol" will help you and your pet avoid serious damage and potential danger.

Both children and adults should learn the proper way to pick up and carry a puppy—one hand supports the rear, the other hand is placed under the chest between the puppy's legs.

Lifting and Carrying Your Bichon

Learning to pick up and carry the bichon puppy properly is very important for both adult and child. You should pick up the puppy with one hand supporting its rear and hindquarters and the other hand under the puppy's chest. This gives the puppy a feeling of security and enables you to keep full control. A puppy should never be picked up by its front legs or by the scruff of the neck.

Only children old enough to safely hold and control a puppy should be allowed to pick it up at all. Puppies can suddenly squirm and attempt to get away. A fall from any height can seriously and permanently injure a puppy.

The New Puppy and Other Pets

The bichon puppy's introduction to older and/or larger dogs in the household must also be carefully supervised.

The average bichon puppy loves the world and all creatures in it. The adult dog "with seniority" however, may consider the new youngster an intrusion and mistake its exuberance as aggression. For this reason it is very important to confine the newcomer so that the older dog is not constantly harassed before it has had time to fully accept the puppy. The partitioned area set up to accommodate the new puppy that we described earlier will give the senior member of the canine contingent an opportunity to inspect the new arrival at leisure without having to endure unsolicited attention.

As mentioned before, bichons are among the most amiable dogs. We have seen them develop lasting friendships with dogs the size of Great Danes and St. Bernards and we have seen other bichons take charge of and become very protective of little creatures like kittens, hamsters, and small birds.

Car Travel

A part of a bichon puppy's socialization process will take place away from home. The puppy must learn to accept strange people and places, and the only way for the puppy to learn to take these changes in stride is to visit as many new sites and meet as many strangers as you can arrange. Trips to the shopping mall or walks through the park will expose your young bichon to new and different situations each time you are out. Of course this should never be attempted until your bichon puppy has had all of its inoculations. Once that is completed, you and your puppy are ready to set off to meet the world. This often involves riding in a car.

Most adult bichons love to ride in a car; the moment they hear those car keys jingle they are ready and willing to go. Some puppies unfortunately suffer varying degrees of motion sickness. The best way to overcome this problem, should it exist, is to begin with very short rides—as short as once around the block. Ending the ride with a fun romp or, should the puppy be interested, a little food treat helps make the ride something to be enjoyed.

When the puppy seems to accept these short rides happily, the length of time in the car can be increased gradually until you see that the young bichon is truly enjoying the outings. Even those dogs and puppies suffering the most severe cases of carsickness seem to respond to this approach and soon begin to consider the car a second home.

Words of Caution on Dogs and Cars

As much as it might seem more enjoyable to have your bichon puppy or adult ride loose in the car, this can be extremely dangerous. An overly enthusiastic canine passenger can interfere with the driver's control or divert the driver's attention. Also a sudden stop can hurl your dog against the front window, severely injuring or even killing it.

The safest way to transport your bichon is in a carrier with the door securely latched. There are also cars such as station wagons that accommodate partitions commonly referred to as "dog guards." These safety devices confine dogs to the rear portion of the car. Employing these simple safety precautions might one day save the life of your pet.

Another important travel tip is to make sure your canine companion is wearing a collar with identification tags attached. In fact, whenever your bichon is not at home with you, it should be wearing a collar with identification tags. Many times dogs are thrown clear of the car in an accident but become so frightened they run blindly away. Not knowing where they are and not carrying any means of identification, the dogs may be lost forever.

It is important that you make it a practice never to leave your bichon alone in the car with the windows closed. Even on cool days the sun beating down on a closed car can send the inside temperature soaring. Though one would expect it to be more the case with black or dark-colored dogs, bichons are extremely heat sensitive. On hot days most bichons will do their best to avoid direct sunlight. To leave a bichon alone in an unventilated car could easily cause its death.

Early Training

Simple basic training should begin just as soon as you bring your puppy home. It must be remembered, however, that a young puppy's attention span is very short and puppies are incapable of understanding or retaining complex commands.

It should also be noted here that bichons as a breed are very sensitive to correction and a scolding is usually sufficient to get your point across. Shaking or striking a bichon is never necessary. Even the most persistent unwanted behavior can normally be taken care of by slapping a rolled up newspaper on the floor and giving a sharp "no!"

Learning the Meaning of "No!"

Probably the most important single command your bichon will ever learn is the word *"no!"* Never use the word unless you are prepared to enforce it. This is the only way the puppy will understand its meaning; once understood, it can and will save both you and the puppy a great deal of unnecessary trauma.

"Come"

The next most important lesson for the puppy to learn is to come when called. It is critical therefore that the puppy become familiar with its name as soon as possible. Learning to come when called could well save your bichon's life when the two of you venture out into the world. "Come" is the command a dog must understand has to be obeyed always and instantly, but the dog should not associate that command with fear. Your bichon's responding to its name and the word "come" should always be associated with a pleasant experience such as great praise and petting or a food treat.

In dog training of any kind it is much easier to avoid establishment of bad habits than it is to correct entrenched, undesirable behavior. Never give the "come" command unless you are sure your bichon puppy will come to you.

Only use the word "no" when you mean to enforce it.

Initially use the command when the puppy is already on its way to you or give the command while walking away from the youngster.

Very young puppies will normally want to stay as close to their owner as possible, especially in strange surroundings. When your puppy sees you moving away, its natural inclination will be to get close to you. This is a perfect time to use the "come" command.

Later, as the puppy grows more independent and perhaps a bit headstrong, you may want to attach a long leash or rope to the puppy's collar to insure the correct response. Chasing or punishing your puppy for not obeying the "come" command in the initial training stages makes the youngster associate the command with something negative and will result in avoidance rather than the immediate positive response you desire. It is imperative that you praise your puppy when it does come to you, even if it delays responding for many minutes.

35

HOW-TO:
Housebreak Your Bichon

Previously we mentioned the great value in getting your bichon accustomed to a wire cage or fiberglass shipping kennel. These containers are commonly called crates by dog breeders. They are invaluable in housebreaking your puppy.

It has been our experience that new dog owners will initially look upon the crate method of confinement during housebreaking as cruel. More often than not, these same people come back to thank us for suggesting the crate method as one of the most valuable training tips they have ever learned. Using a crate reduces the average housebreaking time to a minimum and eliminates keeping the puppy under constant stress by correcting it for making mistakes in the home. Most dogs continue to use their crates voluntarily as a place to sleep, as it provides a sense of safety and security. It becomes their cave or den and in many cases a place to store their favorite toys or bones.

Those of us who live in an earthquake-prone area find our dogs will make a hasty retreat to their crate at the earliest sign of tremor. Often we have found it necessary to become very persistent to get some dogs to emerge from their crate even after the quake has long passed.

Confining your puppy is the only possible way to avoid soiling accidents occurring in the house. Dogs are instinctively clean animals and will not soil their immediate surroundings unless they have no choice.

The Crate Method

The crate used for housebreaking should not be too large or the puppy will sleep at one end and eliminate in the other. The crate should be large enough for the puppy to stretch out comfortably as well as stand up and turn around easily. Naturally this creates a problem in that the proper size crate for an eight-week-old puppy will not be the proper size for a five-month-old puppy. The easiest way to solve this is to use a piece of plywood to block off a part of the crate, adjusting the space accordingly as the puppy grows.

Begin using the crate by feeding the puppy in it. Close and latch the door while the puppy is eating. Just as soon as the food has been consumed, unlatch the crate door and *carry* the puppy outdoors to the place where you want it to eliminate. Should you not have access to the outdoors or feel you will later

The "crate method" of housebreaking can be one of the most valuable training procedures you will use. It reduces housebreaking time to a minimum.

not be able to provide outdoor access for the housebroken dog, place newspapers or some other absorbent material in an out-of-the-way place that will remain easily accessible to the dog. Do not let the puppy run about or play after eating until you have carried it to the designated area. It is extremely difficult to teach a bichon puppy not to eliminate indoors once it has begun to do so. It is very important to prevent accidents rather than correct them.

Young puppies will void both bowel and bladder almost immediately after eating, after strenuous play, and upon waking up from a night's sleep or even a nap. Your being aware of this will save a good many accidents. If, after each of these activities you consistently take the puppy to the place designated for eliminating, you will reinforce the habit of going there for that purpose.

Only after seeing that the puppy has relieved itself in both ways should you allow the puppy to play unconfined and then only while you are there to watch what is happening. Should the puppy begin to sniff the floor and circle around or squat down to relieve itself say "no!," pick it up immediately, and take it to the designated place.

When you are not able to watch what the puppy is doing indoors, it should be in the crate with the door latched. Each time you take the puppy to its crate, throw a small food treat into the crate and praise the puppy as it enters the crate to go after the treat. If the puppy starts whining, barking, or scratching at the door because it wants to be let

A sure sign the young puppy is preparing to relieve itself is when it begins to sniff the floor and circle around or squat.

out, it is crucial that you do not submit to those demands. The puppy must learn not only to stay in its crate but also to do so without complaining unnecessarily.

Every time the puppy begins to whine or bark say "no!" very firmly. If necessary, give the crate a sharp rap with a rolled up newspaper. It may take a good bit of persistence on your part, but patience will win out in the end.

Developing a Schedule

It is important to realize that a puppy of eight to twelve weeks will have to relieve its bladder every few hours except at night. You must adjust your schedule and the puppy's accordingly. You must also be sure your puppy has entirely relieved itself at night just before you retire and be prepared to attend to this the very first thing in the morning when you awake. Just how early in the morning your puppy needs its first outing will undoubtedly be determined by the puppy itself, but do not expect the young puppy to wait very long for you to respond to its "I have

to go out now" signals. You will quickly learn to identify the difference between a puppy's signals that nature is calling and those that indicate it simply does not want to be confined.

Care and persistence in this project pays off very quickly with most bichon puppies, and eventually you will begin to detect a somewhat anxious look or attitude in the puppy that indicates that it needs to relieve itself. Even the slightest indication in this direction should be met with immediate action on your part and accompanied with high praise and positive reinforcement.

When the Owner Is Away All Day

The crate method of housebreaking is without a doubt the simplest and quickest method I have ever found to housebreak the bichon puppy. It is obvious, however, that this method can not be used by someone who is away from the home all day or for even many hours at a time. Young puppies cannot contain themselves for long periods of time. An alternative method must be used, but confinement is still the operative word for success.

A puppy should never be left to roam the house while the owners are away. It is dangerous for the puppy and toilet accidents are bound to happen. The fenced-off area in the kitchen recommended for the arrival of the new puppy is the ideal place of confinement for your puppy while you are gone. The space should be only large enough to permit the puppy to eliminate away from the place in which it sleeps. The entire

Housebreaking
When to Take Your Puppy Outdoors
1. Very first thing in the morning
2. Immediately after eating
3. Immediately after drinking
4. Right after a nap
5. When it circles and sniffs the floor
6. Right after "playtime"
7. When it gets that "perplexed" look
8. When it starts to squat

During the housebreaking process it is important to take your puppy outdoors frequently at regular intervals.

kitchen area is normally too large a space and creates the eliminating at random habit that is to be avoided at all cost.

The floor of the fenced-off area should be lined with newspaper. Roll-end unprinted newspaper stock can be purchased at many print shops and will help to keep your bichon puppy white. The puppy will become accustomed to relieving itself on the newspaper and this should become the "designated spot" to which you will take your puppy when you are home and the puppy indicates it has need to eliminate. When you are home you must insist the puppy use the newspapers every time.

Leash Training

It is never too early to accustom the bichon puppy to a collar and leash. It is your way of keeping your dog under control. It may not be necessary for the puppy or adult bichon to wear its collar and identification tags within the confines of your home and property, but no dog should ever leave home without a collar and without the leash held securely in your hand.

Begin getting your puppy accustomed to its collar by leaving it on for a few minutes at a time. Gradually extend the time you leave the collar on. Most puppies become accustomed to their collar very quickly and forget they are even wearing it.

Once this is accomplished, attach a lightweight leash to the collar while you are playing with the puppy in the house or in your yard. Do not try to guide the puppy at first. The point here is to accustom the puppy to the feeling of having something attached to the collar. Encourage the puppy to follow you as you move away. Should the puppy be reluctant to cooperate, coax it along with a treat of some kind. Hold the treat in front of the puppy's nose to encourage it to follow you. Just as soon as the puppy takes a few steps toward you praise it enthusiastically and continue to do so as you continue to move along.

Make the initial session very brief and very enjoyable. Continue the lessons in your home or yard until the puppy is completely unconcerned about the fact that it is on a leash. With a treat in one hand and the leash in the other you can begin to use both to guide the puppy in the direction you wish to go.

Once the collar and leash are being taken in stride you can begin your walks in front of the house, then down the street, and eventually around the block. You and your bichon puppy are on your way to a lifetime of adventure.

The Adult Bichon

Understanding Your Bichon

Historically the bichon frise has been a close companion to people. Whether pampered in the courts of the nobility, living on the streets with vendors and entertainers, or treasured now as your friend, one thing has remained constant—the bichon is always happiest in the company of its owner. This characteristic has been cultivated and perpetuated through selective breeding over many centuries.

There are some breeds that do well living outdoors in a run or in a kennel with only minimal human contact. The bichon is definitely not one of those breeds. The charming personality and sensitivity for which the breed is noted blossoms with constant human association. If the bichon is left alone too often or for long periods of time, behavioral problems can develop.

It is not unusual to find a perfectly housebroken bichon protest denial of human contact by forgetting all about house manners. Bichons that are not given the attention they need can become frustrated and begin to destroy things. More often than not this destruction focuses on personal objects belonging to the lonely bichon's owner.

This does not mean people who are away at work or school all day can not own a bichon. What it does mean is you must plan on giving your bichon quality attention and affection every day during the hours you are at home. This can come in the form of daily walks, playing retrieving games, grooming sessions, or simply having your bichon sit beside you while you watch television or read in the evening hours.

A Passive Breed

Basically the bichon can best be described as a passive rather than an assertive breed of dog. A more passive dog like the bichon prefers to stay at home or travel with its master and is seldom what is referred to as a "runaway" or "wanderer." Like most passive breeds the bichon thoroughly enjoys exercise but does not become hyperactive and destructive if a day is missed. A bichon barks to sound the alarm but quickly settles down and seldom if ever barks or growls as a sign of aggression.

It is a rare bichon that would challenge its owner on any point. The breed is most comfortable knowing the household rules and having an owner that makes sure the rules are enforced.

Helpful hint: The bichon tries to please in all respects and is relatively easy to train just so long as you avoid being heavy-handed. Bichons are extremely sensitive to correction and a simple scolding is usually more than sufficient to get your point across. Never strike your bichon under any circumstance. There are a good many breeds where a smart slap on the rear quarter with a rolled up newspaper is needed to get their attention if nothing else. The bichon is not a breed where this is necessary or advisable. Should the rolled up newspaper technique ever be used to make a correction, the noise created by slapping the floor with the paper is more than enough to let your bichon know you are displeased.

A happy, healthy and well-trained bichon is always willing to please and does its best to understand your every mood and command. This Champion Bichon has that "what's next?" look in her eye.

Exercise and Outdoor Manners

If your bichon shares its life with another dog or with children, there is every likelihood that it will be getting as much exercise as it needs. Bichons love to romp and play and will attempt to entice almost any human or animal available to join in. In fact, even bichons that have no playmates will invent games that keep their cardiovascular systems in shape and any excess energy in check.

One individual game it seems all bichons enjoy creating is what we call "the bichon racetrack." Our bichons will establish a particular route through the house—possibly around the dining room table, down the hall, through a bedroom, back down the hall to where they started, and around the track again and again. They will do this at top speed as though racing against the fastest competitor imaginable. Once the race has been completed, they will plop down and give us a look of, "Well then, wasn't that a fine race to have won?"

Do not think your bichon would not enjoy a long walk with you every day; to the contrary. Most bichons will willingly walk as far, and perhaps further, than their owners wish to go. Regardless of how many playmates your bichon has at home or how many games it plays on its own, a good brisk walk every day will contribute immensely toward keeping you both happy and healthy.

It is important to understand that while we have referred to the bichon as one of the more passive breeds, we do not mean it is delicate by any means. Don't forget this was a hardy

Even young puppies are quick to learn simple commands like "no" and "come." Basic training should begin just as soon as the puppy arrives in its new home.

street dog for many generations. The breed had to take care of itself in all kinds of weather and in all kinds of situations.

If you and your bichon both keep moving, you need not worry about even the coldest of outdoor weather. The bichon is a tough little breed and its own furry jacket protects it from even freezing temperatures.

On the other hand, caution should be exercised during hot weather. Plan your walks for early morning or after the sun has gone down. Most bichons do not like extremely hot weather and avoid direct sun when temperatures begin to soar.

You must remember to keep your bichon under control at all times when you are out walking. Always use a leash and collar and make sure the

identification tags are securely attached to the collar.

Remember that not all people are dog lovers and even those who are may not like strange dogs jumping up on them on the street. Short leash your bichon as you pass strangers. Only if the person indicates a desire to become more friendly with your dog should you allow your bichon to approach the person.

Never let your dog relieve itself where people might walk or children are playing. Try to teach your bichon to use the gutter to relieve itself. Even then you should always carry a small plastic baggy to remove droppings immediately and dispose of them in a trash receptacle. Many city governments impose heavy fines on dog owners who do not pick up after their dogs.

HOW-TO:
Basic Obedience Training

The "Sit" and "Stay" Commands

Equal in importance to the "no!" command and learning to come when called are the "sit" and "stay" commands. Even puppies can learn the sit command quickly, especially if it appears to be a game and a food treat is involved.

First, it is important to remember that the bichon-in-training be on collar and leash for this and all other lessons. This will avoid the possibility of your bichon's trying to dash off to avoid having to do something it might not want at that moment.

Give the "sit" command immediately before pushing down on your bichon's hindquarters. Praise the dog lavishly when it does sit, even though it is you who made the action take place. A food treat always seems to get the lesson across to your canine student more quickly.

Give the "sit" command just before you push down on your bichon's hindquarters.

Once your puppy has learned the "sit" command you can start working on "stay."

Continue holding your bichon's rear end down, repeating the "sit" command several times. If your dog makes an attempt to get up, repeat the command again while exerting pressure on the rear end until the correct position is maintained. Make your bichon stay in this position for increasing lengths of time. Begin with a few seconds and increase the time as lessons progress over the following weeks.

Any attempt to get up or to lie down should be corrected by saying, "No, sit!" in a firm voice. This should be accompanied by returning the dog to the desired sit position. Only when you decide your dog should get up should it be allowed to do so. When you do decide the dog can get up, call its name, say "OK" and make a big fuss over it. Praise and a food treat are in order every time your dog responds correctly.

Once the "sit" lesson has been mastered, you may start on the "stay" command. With your dog on leash and facing you, command it to sit. Take a step or two back, and if your

dog attempts to get up to follow you say firmly, "Sit, stay!" At the same time raise your hand, palm toward the dog, and again command "Stay!"

Any attempt on your dog's part to get up must be corrected immediately, returning it to the sit position and repeating, "Stay!" Once your bichon begins to understand what it must do, you may gradually increase the distance you step back from a few steps to several yards. Your bichon eventually must learn that the "Sit, stay" commands must be obeyed no matter how far away you are. Later on, with advanced training, your bichon will learn the command is obeyed even when you move entirely out of sight.

As your bichon begins to understand what you wish in this lesson and has remained in the sit position for as long as you have dictated, do not make the mistake of calling the dog to you at first. This makes the dog overly anxious to get up and run to you. Instead walk back to the dog and repeat the "OK" that is a signal that the command is over. Later, when your dog becomes more reliable in this respect, you can call it to you.

The "sit, stay" lesson can take considerable time and patience. We reserve at least the "stay" part of the training until the bichon is at least six months old, because everything in a very young bichon puppy's makeup dictates that, for protection, it get up and follow you wherever you go. Forcing a very young puppy to operate against its natural preservation instincts can be bewildering.

The "Lie Down" Command

Once your bichon has mastered the "sit" and "stay" commands, you may begin work on "lie down." This is especially useful if you want your bichon to remain in a particular place for a long period of time.

Early in the training there can be a little more resistance to obeying the "lie down" command than there was to the "sit" command. Once a bichon has become accustomed to lying down on command it seems to be more relaxing for the dog and it seems less inclined to get up and wander.

With your bichon sitting in front of you and facing you, give the command, "lie down!" Then reach down and slide the dog's front feet toward you. The dog will automatically then be lying down. Again, praise and a food treat are appropriate. Continue assisting your bichon into the "lie down" position until it does so on its own. Be firm and be

Teaching your bichon the "lie down" command may take a bit more patience on your part. However, once mastered this position is more apt to be more relaxing for the dog than maintaining the sit position over extended periods of time.

patient. Obeying this command can take a bit of time before some dogs respond, even when they understand fully what it is you want them to do.

The "Heel" Command

Teaching your bichon to heel is the very basis for off-leash control. In learning to heel, your dog will walk on your left side with its shoulder next to your leg no matter which direction you might go. We do not advocate ever having your dog off leash when away from home, but it is reassuring to know that your dog will obey and stay with you regardless of circumstances.

I have found a lightweight, link-chain training collar is very useful for the heeling lesson. It provides both quick pressure around the neck and a snapping sound, both of which get the dog's attention. Erroneously referred to as a "choke collar," the link-chain collar used properly will not choke the dog.

As soon as your bichon has learned to walk along on the leash, insist that it walk on your left side. A quick short jerk on the leash will keep your dog from lunging from side to side, pulling ahead or lagging back. Always keep the leash slack while your dog maintains the proper position at your side. Should the dog begin to drift away, give the "heel" command followed immediately by a sharp jerk on the leash and guide the dog back to the correct position.

Do not pull on the lead with steady pressure. A sharp but gentle jerking motion is what is needed to get your dog's attention. It is amazing how quickly

Once your bichon has learned the "heel" command, both of you will find your daily walks much more enjoyable.

most bichons will learn to obey the "heel" command.

Training Classes

For obedience work beyond the basic "good canine citizen" training described, it is wise for the bichon owner to seek out local professional assistance. This can be obtained in many ways. There are free-of-charge classes at Department of Parks and Recreation facilities, as well as very formal and sometimes very expensive individual lessons with private trainers. There are some obedience schools that will take your dog and train it for you. We find in the case of bichons that both dog and owner are vastly more successful when they work and train together.

Should you decide to employ the services of a professional dog trainer, it is very important that the trainer be experienced with smaller, more sensitive breeds. A heavy hand does not work with bichons and a stern disciplinarian could ruin your bichon's outgoing temperament forever.

Obedience classes can help you and your bichon to understand each other and you will soon find your classmate looking to you for the commands which let it know what to do next.

Dealing with Problems

Most of the problems owners experience with their bichons are the fault of the owner rather than the dog. One must not forget a bichon is first and foremost a dog, and one of the basic needs of all dogs is to have a "pack leader." A pack leader sets boundaries and in so doing gives the members of the pack a sense of security.

Boundary setting and enforcing those boundaries do not intimidate your dog or diminish its spontaneity. Setting limits actually establishes a line of communication between you and your dog that works for both of you.

The problems that bichon owners may run into are the basic "growing up and learning the rules" situations that most dog owners face. I do not find the bichon particularly destructive or stubborn. If anything, the breed is inclined to be a little bit lazy about rules, ignoring them if not consistently enforced.

Chewing: It is important not to confuse your dog. A dog cannot tell the difference between your discarded old slipper and your newest pair of dress shoes. Both smell exactly like you and are just as chewable. Don't expect your dog to understand that it is OK to chew on one and not the other. Never give your dog any of your personal items to chew on; you must assist the dog's learning that none of the smell-just-like-you items is a plaything.

Dogs chew things because they enjoy it. Chewing relieves stress and boredom. Half the battle is in preventing dogs from chewing the wrong things. Don't give your dog the opportunity to do so. Make sure the dog is confined to its crate or dog-proof room with something OK to chew when you are not there to supervise. Sound cruel? Think again. Which is more cruel, safely confining your dog when you are not there or flying into a rage because the dog entertained itself by eating a hole in the sofa while you were gone?

Housebreaking problems: Housebreaking is based upon a dog's natural dislike for eliminating where it eats and sleeps. Again, supervision is your greatest asset here. A dog does not have to eliminate near its food or sleeping place when given the freedom of the whole house. The housebreaking process is dealt with in detail elsewhere in this book, but this is a reminder of the value of confinement and routine in this respect.

Jumping up: Even people who do like dogs do not particularly like to be jumped upon when they enter someone's home. Consistency is the only thing that works here. Do not let your dog jump up on your leg or on anyone else's—ever. A leg is a leg, and if it is OK to jump up on yours for a pat, then in the dog's mind, all other legs are fair game as well.

When your bichon runs joyfully to greet you and jumps up for a pat, give the command "off!" and push its paws off your leg. Just as soon as the dog's paws hit the floor, praise it lavishly. Everyone in the family must do this or it will not work. When you and your dog are away from home, have your dog under control on its leash and repeat the command when your dog attempts to jump up on strangers.

Fear of being alone: Dogs are social creatures and some become more upset at being left alone than others. They may bark, whine, or attempt to destroy things. All dogs must learn that your absence is simply a matter of routine. Don't treat your departure or return like the climax in a romance novel. Dogs get caught up in your emotional responses. If the dog relates your coming and going with hugging, kissing, and all kinds of heightened emotion, it upsets its dependent nature and creates anxiety.

Feeling secure in the kennel or cage you have provided is the first step in your dog's "home alone" training. This nips in the bud any chance of destructive behavior. Going in and out of the room while the dog is confined is the next stage. The dog is learning that you do come back.

Stepping outside the house but remaining within earshot comes next. The minute the barking or howling begins, you must command "no!"

Increase the time you are out of sight but not out of earshot. Eventually your absence will go by unnoticed. This may take longer to accomplish with some dogs than it does with others, but persistence is the key. When being left alone is no longer a traumatic experience, you can experiment with leaving the dog loose in a room or in the house if you wish, but again, this should be done gradually.

Digging: Dogs like to dig. They do it to relieve boredom and to find a nice cool spot to lie in. Perhaps the bichon's ancient barbet heritage make the breed particularly fond of dirt, mud, and water, but whatever the reason, like it they do. Correcting the digging problem is not easy.

Again, supervision works best. If it is not possible to supervise your dog while it is outdoors, keep it in until you can be there to watch what is going on. The minute your dog attempts to dig, let it know—with that tried and true "no" command—that this is not acceptable. Good luck on this one!

Spaying and Neutering

All companion bichons, whether male or female, should be sexually altered unless specifically purchased to breed or to show. Only a bichon purchased from a breeder who has recommended that it be bred should be allowed to have offspring. You would be astounded how many dogs and cats, numbering in the millions, that are put to sleep each year because they have no homes.

I trust that you, as a responsible dog owner, would never allow your bichon to roam the streets, nor would you consider turning it over to the dog pound. Yet there is no way you can guarantee that someone who might purchase a puppy from you will not be irresponsible and permit the dog to roam or to wind up being euthanized at the pound.

Parents who wish to have their young children "experience the miracle of birth" can do so by renting videos of animals giving birth. Handling the experience this way saves adding to the serious pet overpopulation.

There is constant lobbying throughout America to restrict the rights of all dog owners and dog breeders because of this pet overpopulation and the unending need to destroy unwanted animals. Thoughtful dog owners will leave the breeding process to experienced individuals who have the facilities to keep all resulting offspring on their premises until suitable and responsible homes can be found.

Altering your pet can also avoid some of the more distasteful aspects of dog ownership. As previously discussed, males that have not been altered have the natural instinct to lift their legs and urinate on objects to mark the territory in which they live. It is extremely difficult to teach an unaltered male not to do this in your home.

The female bichon will have her two estrus cycles that are accompanied by a bloody discharge. Unless the female is kept confined there will be extensive soiling of the area in which she is allowed.

Toys

The rules for selecting toys for the bichon puppy apply throughout the lifetime of your dog. Never give a bichon a toy that is small enough to fit in the dog's mouth or which can be chewed apart into small pieces.

Some bichons treasure teddy bears and other stuffed animals and keep them nearly intact for many years; however, toys of this kind can be dangerous. Any buttons or eyes should be removed from the stuffed toy at once, and play with these stuffed animals should take place only when and where it can be supervised. More than one dog has expressed its displeasure at being left behind by completely dismantling a favorite teddy bear or stuffed doll. The danger here is that the material with which the toy has been stuffed can be ingested and cause severe illness or even death.

Good Behavior

Responsible owners will have begun training when their bichon arrived. Trying to undo bad habits is extremely difficult for the trainer and very bewildering for a dog. For instance, a dog that has been permitted to sleep on its master's bed or climb up on furniture for many months can simply not understand why, starting today, this is no longer allowable. You may well have a good reason for making this change, but you will be hard pressed to make your bichon understand the reason. What will result instead is a constant war; your bichon will do everything in its power to resume its comfortable habit, and you will lose patience with its attempts to do so.

If your bichon's first attempts to break any household rule is met with a sharp *"no!"* it is highly unlikely the issue will become a contest of wills. We cannot emphasize enough the value in avoiding rather than correcting bad habits.

Feeding Your Bichon

Your bichon can be put on an adult feeding schedule at about ten months of age. This means the adult bichon will receive one main meal a day, preferably at the same time each evening. This meal is supplemented by a morning snack, and for this we highly recommend hard dog biscuits. These not only prove to be a much anticipated treat, but do wonders toward maintaining healthy gums and teeth.

The correct amount of food to maintain a bichon's optimum condition varies as much from dog to dog as it does from human to human. Much depends upon how much your bichon exercises. A dog that is given a sedate walk once or twice a day and is otherwise confined to a small apartment is going to require far less food than a dog that has the freedom to run an entire house or yard. On the other hand, a bichon that has a rough-and-ready canine companion or one that frolics with young children all day will need considerably more food than the more sedentary dog.

The correct amount of food for a normally active bichon is that which it will eat readily within about fifteen minutes of being given the meal. What your dog does not eat in that amount of time should be taken up and discarded. Leaving food out for extended periods of time can lead to erratic and finicky eating habits.

While some breeds of dogs will eat as much as you will give them and become obese, this is seldom the case with a bichon. In our many years of involvement with the breed, we have seen only one or two bichons that one would consider seriously overweight.

Unfortunately, it is not unusual to find the opposite to be true. Some bichons can become very picky eaters. This is usually brought about by overly solicitous owners who panic at their dog's first refusal of food and begin to hand feed or tempt it to eat by offering expensive and often totally nonnutritious treats.

Fresh water and a properly prepared balanced diet containing the essential nutrients in correct proportions is all a healthy dog needs to be offered. If your bichon will not eat the food offered, it is because it is either not hungry or not well. If the former is the case, the dog will eat when it is hungry. If you suspect the latter, an appointment with your veterinarian is in order.

Canned Food or Dry?

A great deal of research is conducted by manufacturers of the leading brands of dog food to determine the

Whether you are choosing canned or dry food read labels carefully. The main ingredient should be derived from meat, poultry or fish.

Dry dog food is the most economical, but least tasty choice.

exact ratio of vitamins and minerals necessary to maintain your dog's well-being. This applies to both canned and dry foods, but like most other things in life, "you get what you pay for." It costs the manufacturer more to produce a nutritionally balanced, high-quality food that is easily digested by a dog than it does to produce a brand that provides only marginal nourishment.

By law, every container of dog food must list all the ingredients in descending order by weight. The major ingredient is listed first, the next most prominent follows, and so on down the line.

A diet based on meat or poultry (appearing first in the ingredients list) is going to provide more nutrition per pound of food than one that lists a filler grain product as major ingredient. The diet based on meat and poultry will also cost more than a food heavy in inexpensive fillers.

Dogs, whether Chihuahuas or Great Danes, are carnivorous (meat-eating) animals, and while vegetable content of your dog's diet should not be overlooked, a dog's physiology and anatomy are based upon carnivorous food acquisition. Protein and fat are absolutely essential to a dog's well-being. The animal protein and fat your dog needs can be replaced by some vegetable proteins, but the amounts and the kind require a clear understanding of nutrition.

There are so many excellent commercial dog foods available today that it seems a waste of time, effort, and money to try to duplicate the nutritional content of these carefully thought-out products by cooking food from scratch. It is important though that you read labels carefully or consult with your veterinarian, who will assist you in selecting the best moist or dry food for your bichon.

Whether canned or dry, look for a food in which the main ingredient is derived from meat, poultry, or fish. Remember, you cannot purchase a top-quality dog food for the same price as one that lacks the nutritional value you are looking for. In many cases you will find your bichon not only needs less of the better food, but there will be less fecal waste as well.

Special Diets

A good number of dog-food manufacturers now produce special diets for overweight, underweight, and aged dogs. The calorie content of these foods is adjusted to suit the particular problem that accompanies each of these conditions.

There is no better remedy for these conditions, however, than using good, common sense. Too many calories and too little exercise will increase weight. Fewer calories reduces weight. The adult bichon that is underweight would probably do well on a diet specially developed for puppies, because it is much higher in caloric content.

The aged dog needs a much lower-calorie diet than the growing puppy or even adult bichon. It is also important to make sure your older bichon gets some moderate exercise each day.

The old-timer may prefer to spend most of its day on the sofa or comfortable pillow, but moderate exercise will keep your friend alive much longer.

Helpful hints: The better foods are not normally manufactured to look like products that appeal to humans. A dog does not care that a food looks like a sirloin steak or a wedge of cheese. All a dog cares about is how food smells and tastes. The "looks like" dog foods are manufactured to tempt the dog's owner, but since it is highly unlikely that you will be eating your dog's food, do not waste your money.

Be aware of canned or moist products that have the look of "rich red beef" or dry food that is red in color. In most cases the color put there to appeal to you is achieved through the use of red dye. This dye may not be toxic, but dye is dye, and it will stain the hair around your bichon's mouth.

A good red dye test is to place a small amount of canned or well-moistened dry food on a piece of white paper towel. Let the food sit there for about a half hour and then check to see if the towel has been stained. If the toweling has taken on a red stain you can rest assured your bichon's facial hair will do the same.

It's not the look of food that excites your dog, it's the taste and the smell.

Traveling with Your Bichon

At first thought, having your bichon accompany you on an extended trip may sound like great fun for both of you. Further consideration could well alter your decision. You must ask yourself where your bichon will stay when you stop along the way to eat or to sleep. Unlike most European countries, restaurants in America do permit dogs to accompany their masters inside the establishment. Leaving your dog in a parked automobile while you eat can be very dangerous, as weather conditions can change rapidly and temperatures in a closed car can soar.

Leaving the windows open puts your pet in danger of escaping or being stolen, even if it is safely secured in a traveling container. A slightly open window is of little help once the sun begins to beat down on the car.

Many hotels and motels do not allow dogs into the rooms because other guests have abused this privilege in the past. Many of the hotels and motels that do allow pets into the rooms charge an extra fee or security deposit. These establishments also assume that your dog is accustomed to being left alone in a strange place and will not disturb other guests by barking and howling while you are out of your room.

Changing your bichon's accustomed food and water can create a number of problems, including diarrhea. The latter is not something most people wish to cope with while traveling.

When You Do Travel Together

It should be easy to see that taking your bichon along with you on a trip will require a great deal of advance planning. An air-conditioned car can help considerably if your trip will be made through areas where daytime temperatures are high. Take the crate or cage that you have been using at home as well. This keeps your pet safe while traveling and provides a safe, secure, and familiar place if you are out of your hotel room.

Stops along the way must be carefully planned. Realize that your selection of restaurants will have to be made with your pet's safety in mind. At any stop your car must not be left in the sun. Further, unless the weather is very cool, windows should be left open and your car must be where you or a member of your party can see it at all times.

Many people who travel with their pets make an early morning stop at a grocery store or carry-out restaurant and purchase their own food for the day. Meal stops can then be made at some shady spot along the way. Should you decide to do this, it will also give you an opportunity to exercise your dog at the same time.

Dinner should come after you have checked into your hotel or motel and put your dog in your room. Reservations must be made in advance with those places allowing dogs in the rooms. If you have taken our previous advice and trained your bichon to stay alone in its kennel or cage, a

Can I go too? You will be amazed at how quickly your bichon will learn those jangling keys can mean a ride in the family auto.

good part of your problem will be solved. You will not have to worry about barking and howling while you are gone, nor will you run the risk of having your dog cause any damage to the room.

If you have not accustomed your dog to being left alone in its kennel, it is to be hoped that it has at least learned to be left alone. If so, we seriously advise closing your bichon in the bathroom while you are out of the room. It is also wise to leave a "do not disturb" sign on your door while you are gone to avoid a staff person's entering your room and allowing your dog to escape.

If your dog will not stay alone in a strange room without barking, *do not leave it alone!* The dog can become frenzied and destroy things or disturb the other occupants of the hotel. You must be considerate of others—both people who are not particularly dog-tolerant and those who might wish to stay at the same hotel later with their own dog. The management of the hotel will not be disposed to allow other people with dogs to stay if you have abused your privileges.

You must take along an adequate supply of your bichon's accustomed food and water. Changing diets and water can seriously upset your dog, and diarrhea and vomiting are the last things you will want to deal with on your trip.

Do take a brush, comb, and scissors. If you plan to hike or walk your dog along the side of the road, these accessories will enable you to get rid of any unwanted weeds, seeds, or dirt your bichon's coat might have attracted.

Your Aging Bichon

The bichon ages remarkably well, and though lifespan does vary from dog to dog, it is not unusual to find many members of this breed alive and well even at twelve to fourteen years of age. Some of these same old-timers have maintained their sight and hearing and all their teeth until their final days!

Exercise

There are certain precautions that must be taken with the aged bichon to keep it happy and healthy. Exercise must be adjusted as your bichon gets older and you must take pains to see that it is not pushed beyond its capacity when hiking or playing. This is especially so if there are any signs of arthritis and if exercise makes the old boy or girl limp.

Even the aging bichon can remain an enjoyable companion to everyone in the family if the old timer is given a little special consideration.

Diet

Your bichon's diet must also be adjusted accordingly so that there is less strain on the digestive system. The fat content of the food must be reduced. Today most major dog food manufacturers take canine aging into consideration and offer diets specifically geared to the senior citizen.

If your bichon has been accustomed to one major meal each day it is probably wise to adjust this to two smaller meals. It is also absolutely necessary to avoid overweight in the aging dog. The strain of additional weight will certainly shorten its lifespan.

Health Problems

Aging frequently affects the bichon's ability to hear and see. If you find your previously obedient bichon failing to respond quickly or not at all to your call, do make concessions for age.

Also the old bichon's patience may wear thin much more quickly than it did when it was a youngster. Puppies and children can prove extremely tiresome to the elderly bichon and it is up to the owner not to allow the old-timer to be subjected to youthful harassment.

It is not uncommon for some older bichons to develop diabetes and kidney stones. These conditions are treatable by your veterinarian. Diabetes requires insulin injections on a daily basis. A veterinarian can show you how these inoculations can be administered.

Excessive drinking of water can be a sign that the kidneys are not working properly. In some cases this can be a sign that bitches that have not been

Exercise must be adjusted as your dog gets older. The dog must not be pushed beyond its limits.

spayed are developing pyrometra, which is an inflammation of the womb. This is a condition that requires prompt professional treatment.

Veterinary science has developed many new methods which assist your dog to stay healthy even through its final years. Regular checkups will prevent rapid progress of the ailments that could lead to the deterioration of your pet.

The Last Goodbye

There will come a time however, when your canine friend of many years is no longer able to enjoy life and you must make a very heart-wrenching decision. Fortunately when science is no longer able to prevent our canine friends' suffering or incontinence, we are able to mercifully bring their lives to a close.

Your veterinarian will tell you when the time has come to do this and is able to perform this final act with tenderness and skill. Done professionally, there is no stress to your dog, especially if you are there to hold the dog while the veterinarian administers the injection.

This is never an easy decision to make, but carefully considered, it is the kindest action you can take for your canine friend who has given you so many years of companionship and enjoyment.

Bathing and Grooming

Care of the Puppy Coat

Most breeders begin to accustom a bichon puppy to being groomed and trimmed as soon as it has enough hair to brush. By the time your puppy is ready to come home with you it undoubtedly will have become used to being held to have its nails trimmed, its ears cleaned, and to sitting still long enough to have preliminary trimming around the eyes, under the tail, and so forth.

We would certainly question the reliability of the kennel involved if your puppy was not exposed to these preliminary trimming steps by the time it was ready to go home with you. If this should be the case, however, you must begin these grooming lessons immediately. The older a bichon puppy has grown without learning to accept

This bichon has its own home beauty salon: (left to right) pin brush, slicker brush, medium/fine comb, cotton swabs for ear cleaning, nail clippers, hemostat, hair scissors, shampoo and hair dryer.

grooming procedures, the more frightened it will be initially of what you are attempting to do. Regardless of the amount of resistance your bichon puppy may put up, remember it is objecting to something it does not like, not to something that will harm it.

Grooming is a part of every dog's life and it is a major factor in keeping your bichon clean, healthy, and looking like a bichon. Begin gently but firmly to accustom the new puppy to these procedures. A few minutes are sufficient at first; gradually increase the length of time.

Do not attempt to accomplish your grooming efforts on the floor. The puppy will only attempt to get away and you will spend half your time chasing the unwilling youngster around the room. Buy or build a small grooming table of a height that allows you to stand or sit comfortably while you work. Adjustable-height grooming tables are available at most pet shops. The size of the top of the grooming table should be just large enough for an adult bichon to stand or lie down upon, no larger.

Although brushing the bichon puppy will not take a particularly long time, the situation will be quite different when your bichon has grown up and developed a mature coat. The two of you are going to spend considerable time at the grooming table, so you might as well start early to teach your puppy to lie down on the table and enjoy all the attention it is getting. This is also a good time and place to practice the "sit" and "lie down" lessons.

A prominent part of the look of the bichon frise as a breed is its "powder

Necessary Grooming Supplies

Grooming table—with a rubber mat top to keep the dog from slipping. The table must be firm and steady and of a height that permits you to work comfortably.

Hair dryer—to be used to brush dry your bichon immediately after its bath.

Pin brush—for body coat from the time it reaches any considerable length. The pin brush has long, pliable metal bristles or "pins" set in a cushioned rubber base and is ideal for bichon coats, as it does not pull out the undercoat.

Slicker brush—for puppy coats and shorter coats and for legs and feet of longer-coated dogs. This is an oblong metal brush with a handle. The metal teeth are bent and are set in rubber. This brush should be used sparingly and gently on the adult bichon's coat, as it will pull out the undercoat you are trying to protect if used without care.

Medium/fine comb—the teeth on this comb (often called a "greyhound comb") are divided in half, part being set very close together and the other half set wider. This comb is used for beard, head, and tail and to lift body coat while trimming.

Hemostat or tweezers—for removing hair from the inside of ears, an important part of grooming.

Barber's haircutting shears—specifically designed for haircutting. The better the scissors, the more professional looking the trim job will be.

Nail clippers—designed specifically for trimming your dog's nails.

puff" coat. This coat type is of course a good part hereditary, but proper grooming procedures keep the coat looking as it should.

The coat of a bichon puppy is nothing like what it will be when the puppy reaches maturity. Puppy hair is finer, softer, and very wispy if allowed to grow without being cut back (called "tipping"). Tipping simply means you are cutting back your puppy's coat a small amount all over except for the ear fringes, mustache, beard, and tail. These are the areas that require length rather than any amount of texture.

Some time between nine and twelve months of age you will note that your bichon's coat will consistently mat and tangle, especially if you have not been diligent in keeping the coat tipped and brushed. At this point you will note that a thick, soft undercoat is beginning to develop close to the skin while the outer coat is still silky and sparse. This undercoat is what will hold up the adult hair and help create that "powder puff" look so typical of the bichon. The appearance of this undercoat tells you your puppy is passing into adolescence and its adult coat is beginning to develop.

It is hoped that you and your puppy have worked out any difficulties you may have had surrounding grooming and trimming, because constant care and brushing during this coat change period is critical to avoid matting. From now on your bichon should be brushed at least two or three times a week. Never allow a mat to go unattended. Regular brushing will remove the dead puppy hair before it has a chance to create mats and will encourage the growth of the new hair. Use the pin brush to do this. The slicker brush may be used on the hair of the legs and to separate hair around a mat. If you do use the slicker brush on the body coat or longer hair of the head and tail, do so with extreme care and only by separating the coat into layers and carefully brushing from the root of the hair out, being careful not to pull out undercoat. Never drag the slicker brush over the top of the hair.

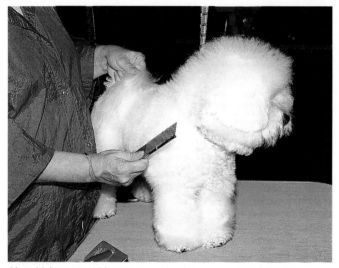

Your bichon should learn to stand quietly on a grooming table. Brushing and trimming is a lifetime affair with this breed and cooperation on the part of the dog is very important.

Bathing

Preparing for the bath: Never bathe a matted bichon! Your efforts will only result in more and larger mats. Prior to bathing, the coat must be brushed out completely and thoroughly with the pin brush. Do not neglect the hard-to-reach areas between the front legs, under the front legs where they join the body, and between the rear legs. Should you find mats, it is not necessary to cut them out. Sprinkle baby powder or grooming powder made for that purpose into the coat and brush completely from the skin out. Help to separate the mat with your fingers, taking care not to tear the hair loose.

Brushing must be done thoroughly and gently. What is referred to as "line-brushing" is undoubtedly the best method. This method requires your bichon to be lying down on its side. Starting at the dog's spine and where the hind leg joins the body, part the hair in a straight line down to the abdomen. Take your left hand and hold down the hair on the left side of the part. Brush through the hair to the right of the part that is not held down. You will be brushing to your right.

Next, make another part about 2 inches (5 cm) to the left and parallel to the first part that you made, and again brush gently through the hair that is not held down. Proceed on toward the front of the dog, continually repeating the parting process until you reach the head. Then turn your dog over on its other side and repeat the process. This same method can be used on the top of the head, chest, legs, and the longer furnishings as well.

When you are finished you will have gone over every square inch of the dog and it will be totally free of mats and tangles. When doing the longer hair on the tail and ears, be very gentle, as this hair seems to be extremely fragile and easily broken and pulled loose. The only hair that you want to remove anywhere on the dog is dead hair that has already come loose.

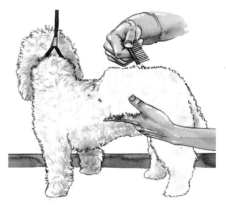

This bichon has been trained to stand for its grooming session. Teaching your dog it must behave during this important process will make the procedure enjoyable for both dog and owner.

Only under extreme circumstances (such as the coat's being entirely matted to the skin) should you ever consider shaving your bichon. The coat serves as insulation against both heat and cold. Misguided owners feel they are doing their dog a service by shaving it in the summer, when exactly the opposite is true.

The inquisitive nature of the bichon will undoubtedly result in mini-disasters at one time or another. Gum, tar, and other foreign substances will find their way into your dog's coat, but it is seldom necessary to cut the hair to correct the problem.

There are many home remedies we have used to cope with such accidents, but the best we have found is a lotion called Avon Skin So Soft, which can be purchased at your local drugstore. Saturate the affected area of the coat with the lotion and allow it to penetrate the foreign substance. The lotion will loosen the gum or tar and you will be able to slide it off with little or no damage to the hair. Repeat if necessary, and when the substance has been entirely removed, wash and rinse the area thoroughly or give the dog a complete bath.

Helpful hint: The inner ear and nails, should be taken care of at this time as well. Once your bichon is in the tub you can attend to cleaning the anal glands also. Doing so while the dog is in the tub allows you to flush the foul-smelling excretion down the drain immediately. Refer to the section on "Home Health Care" for more details.

Be firm but gentle when placing your bichon in the tub. Most bichons will not object to their bath but there are always those that mistrust anything new or strange and will do their best to avoid having to endure it. Since this is a breed that will spend a good portion of its life in the tub, cooperation is essential. Again—be firm but gentle.

Bathing Equipment Needed

Rubber mat—to be placed on bottom of sink or tub to avoid your dog's slipping

Rubber spray hose—for thorough wetting and rinsing

Shampoo—especially made for white dogs

Mineral oil or Vaseline—a drop or small dab applied directly to each eye to protect the eyes from soap irritation

Cotton balls—one in each ear to protect the inner ear from water

Large towel—bath size to be used for partial drying

Hair dryer—for "blow drying" the freshly bathed bichon

Your bichon should be wet down completely with the rubber spray hose using warm, not hot, water. Shampoo and wash well, using extra shampoo on stained or extra dirty areas, particularly on the beard, legs, and tail. Read

It is extremely important to be sure your bichon is mat free before it is bathed. Once a mat is soaked it will become practically impossible to unravel.

Most bichons enjoy their bath if introduced to the process gently. Be careful not to get soap in your bichon's eyes or nose.

shampoo directions carefully; some are concentrated and need to be diluted before using. Others contain bluing agents and should be left on the dog only for a specific length of time.

When using medicated shampoos, spot test to see if the product stains your bichon's coat. If the product does stain, check with your groomer or veterinarian to see if there is a substitute product that will not discolor your bichon's coat.

Start behind the ears and work back. Then return to the head and carefully shampoo and rinse this area. Dogs, like humans, will react strongly to having soap rubbed into their eyes, nose, or mouth, so wash the head area carefully.

Soap should be rinsed out immediately. Repeat the entire process, and this time place special emphasis on final rinsing. You can't rinse too much. Soap left in the coat can cause mats and skin irritation.

With the dog still in the tub, squeeze as much water out of the coat as you can. Then wrap your dog in the towel you have nearby and carry the dog to your grooming table. Here you will towel dry to remove excess moisture in preparation for brush drying.

Drying

Immediately after a quick towel drying, brush through the damp coat quickly with the pin brush. This will remove any tangles created while bathing or in the preliminary towel drying.

Employing the hair dryer and pin brush, you will then commence with the brush drying process. Set your hair dryer at "medium" setting. The "hot" setting may be quicker but it can dry out the hair shafts, causing them to split. You must also be careful not to burn the skin of your bichon with a dryer that is too hot.

Brush drying is the only way you can get the bichon's coat to stand out from the body and achieve the "powder puff" look of the breed. Allowing the bichon's hair to dry on its own without employing the use of a hair dryer and brush will allow the hair to curl up. You will not be able to scissor smoothly to get that plush powder puff look if you allow the hair to curl.

It is best to begin the shampoo and wash just behind the ears and work back to the tail. Then return to the head and carefully wash that area using a soft washcloth.

Actually the "line brushing" method you used before the bath is the best way to brush dry as well, except that it is best to begin at the head and neck with the dog lying on its stomach. Point your dryer at the area to be brushed, using light strokes repeatedly until that section is completely dry, then move on to the next section. With each section of damp hair, use the pin brush to make the part and the slicker brush to do the final drying and straightening. Again, be careful not to pull hair out.

After you have completed the head and neck, follow your line brushing process with the dog lying on its side. You must be sure to dry and brush thoroughly under the legs where they join the body and between the legs. Any hair left to dry on its own, especially in the hard-to-get places, is sure to mat.

Once your bichon is completely dry, you must begin the trimming process immediately. If trimming is delayed, the hair begins to curl and all your brush-drying efforts will have been useless.

Helpful hint: Investing in a dryer that has a stand can be a great help in brush drying. This will allow you to direct the flow of air to where it is needed and will free both your hands to attend to brushing.

Scissoring

The main difference between the pet trim and the correct show trim is primarily in the length of hair, but the details of the show trim are far more complex. The pet trim is much shorter and easier to maintain. The attractive show trim takes a great deal more care to keep up and the long hair collects leaves and twigs if your bichon has regular access to the outdoors.

If you are serious about showing your bichon, at least initially you will have to employ the services of a professional who is an expert at trimming

Squeeze out excess water from your dog's coat while the dog is still in the tub. Then, using a heavy towel quickly pat the coat to remove as much remaining water as you can before you begin to blow dry the coat.

bichons for the show ring. Few grooming parlors are capable of doing this.

If dog shows are in the future of your bichon, you should ask your breeder for a recommendation or attend a dog show in your area.

Brush drying the bichon coat is the only way that you can get the hair to stand out directly from the body in preparation for scissoring.

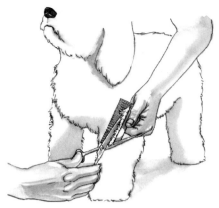

Lift the hair directly away from the body with your comb and scissor a little bit at a time trying to get as smooth a finish as possible. Round the legs off so they resemble cylinders. The hair on the foot should cover the nails.

Learning to handle a comb properly is another important step in dealing with the bichon coat. Learn to lift the hair up, away from the body before any hair is cut.

There will undoubtedly be people showing their bichons who will be able to assist you.

Later as you become more experienced and have ample opportunity to practice, you will be able to learn to trim your bichon for the ring yourself. The standard of the breed is very specific about how the bichon should be groomed for showing, but there are helpful charts and instruction booklets obtainable from the Bichon Frise Club of America.

The decision you make regarding a show career for your bichon will determine how liberal you can be in regard to your dog's play and exercise. The bichon coat is relatively sturdy and can handle normal rough-and-tumble play with other dogs. If the other dogs like to chew on your dog's coat, obviously you are going to have a problem. Your dog will still be able to accompany you on walks and hikes, but a roll in wet green grass can easily stain the coat.

Notice there is no indentation made in the hair at the top of the bichon's ear as is done in a poodle trim. The overall rounded look is a hallmark of the bichon frise breed.

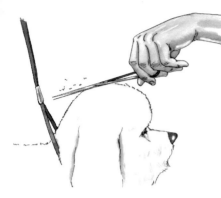

Round off the hair from the eyes to the back of the neck. Remember the bichon's coat is rounded off from every direction.

Whether your dog is destined for the show ring or will spend its entire life at home with you, a bichon is a white, long-coated dog that will need special care if you want it to look anything like the attractive picture that made you originally interested in the breed.

Proper Use of the Comb

Learning proper use of the comb while trimming will assist you greatly in achieving the desired results. Constantly lift the hair up and out as you go along. This process keeps all the hairs standing directly away from the dog's body, and with practice you will be able to achieve that smooth but plush look you are after.

Again, remember that the hair of the beard, ears, and tail is always left much longer than the rest of the coat. The actual length depends upon whether the bichon is being trimmed for the show ring or as a companion.

Helpful hint: It is very important to note that in trimming the head of the bichon, the objective is to create a rounded look. There should be no indentation where the ears join the head as you might see in a poodle trim.

This Champion Bichon is presented perfectly trimmed and groomed by its professional handler.

Veterinary Care

Your veterinarian will prescribe the proper series of inoculations for your bichon. It is extremely important that you obtain a shot record when purchasing your dog so that your veterinarian will know what inoculations have been given previously.

Minor accidents and illnesses will undoubtedly occur while your bichon progresses through puppyhood, adolescence, and on into old age. This chapter is written in the hope that it will assist the owner of a pet bichon to determine the difference between situations that can easily be taken care of at home and those that demand veterinary treatment.

There is one piece of advice that always applies. If you are in doubt about the seriousness of your bichon's problem, do not hesitate to pick up the phone and call your veterinarian. In most cases veterinarians know which questions to ask and will be able to thereby determine whether or not it is necessary to see your dog.

Major Illnesses

Very effective vaccines have been developed to combat diseases that once were fatal to practically any infected dog. The danger of your bichon's being infected with distemper, hepatitis, hard pad, leptospirosis, or the extremely virulent parvovirus is highly unlikely if proper inoculations and booster shots have been given regularly.

Rabies among well-cared for dogs is practically unheard of, but dogs that come in contact with animals in nature can be at risk if not immunized. On occasion, however, there are dogs that, for one reason or another, do not develop full immunity.

Immunization against these infectious diseases begins in puppyhood, and it is extremely important that you follow your veterinarian's inoculation schedule. Neglecting to do so could easily cost your bichon's life.

It is important to recognize the early symptoms of these diseases should your dog be one of the unfortunate few that has not developed complete immunity. Any marked change in your dog's behavior should be observed very closely. This is especially so if your dog is under a year of age.

Should your bichon suddenly become listless, refuse food, and start to cough and sneeze, contact your veterinarian at once. Other signs of possible problems in this area are marked increase in thirst, blood in the stools or urine, and discharge of any kind from the nose.

Accidents

Injuries sustained in a road accident can be fatal if not handled correctly and promptly. If your bichon is struck by an automobile or motorcycle, it is important that you remain calm. Panic on your part will serve only to upset the injured animal and could cause it to thrash about and injure itself even more seriously.

If your dog is unable to move, immediately remove it from the street where it could be further injured. In picking up your injured dog it is critical that you support the body as fully as possible. The less movement of the injured area the better. Do not wait to determine the extent of injury. Internal injuries may have occurred that you are unable to observe immediately. Get the injured dog to a veterinarian without delay. Ask someone to drive you there so that you are free to hold your injured dog and keep it calm. If there is no one else available to drive you, put the injured dog in a container of some kind to keep it as immobile as possible.

Bleeding Wounds
If there is a bleeding wound due to a traffic accident or any other accident, deal with the bleeding at once. Using a pad of cotton or a compress soaked in cold water, apply pressure directly to the bleeding point. If the flow of blood is not stemmed, your dog could bleed to death.

Bichons seldom pick fights with other dogs, but their friendly attitude can spark hostility on the part of other more aggressive dogs. Should your bichon be attacked by another dog, get the two dogs apart as quickly as you can and get your dog to the vet without delay. Bite wounds are invari-ably infected and antibiotic treatment is necessary.

Kennel Cough
Kennel cough (infectious rhinotra-cheitis), while highly infectious, is not a serious disease; it is like a mild case of influenza in humans. It is caused by a mixture of a bacteria and a virus. The name of the disease is misleading in that it implies that a dog must be in a kennel environment to be infected. Actually it is very easily passed from one dog to another in almost any situation.

The symptoms can make the disease sound far worse than it actually is. We find the symptoms particularly nerve-wracking, because there is a persistent hacking cough that at times makes one think surely the dog will bring up everything it has ever eaten!

There are various protective procedures now available that can be administered by your veterinarian. In addition to inoculations, there is an intranasal vaccine. These protective measures are advisable for your bichon if you ever take it to a dog park or plan on placing it in a boarding kennel. Many boarding kennels now insist upon proof of protection against kennel cough before they will allow a dog to be admitted.

Bladder Stones
It is yet to be determined if this is an inherited problem in the bichon, but it is a disease known to this and many other small breeds. Bladder stones form when excess minerals and other waste products crystallize in the bladder.

Symptoms are difficult and frequent urination, blood in the urine, general weakness, and loss of appetite. Immediate veterinary care must be sought if any of these symptoms is observed, because untreated the condition can cause severe and permanent kidney damage and even death in extreme cases.

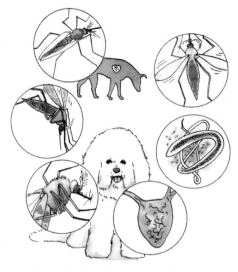

Life cycle of the heartworm: infected mosquitoes bite your dog and deposit the heartworm larvae on its skin. The larvae enter the bloodstream through the hole created by the mosquito bite and make their way to the dog's heart.

Life cycle of the tapeworm: fleas are commonly hosts of the tapeworm. When the flea is swallowed the parasite is shared with your dog, tapeworms develop and segments are passed in the feces.

Internal Parasites

Tapeworms and heartworms are best diagnosed and treated by your veterinarian. Great advances are continually made in dealing with both these parasites and what was once a complicated and time-consuming treatment has been simplified over the years.

Tapeworms: Tapeworms are a part of the life cycle of the flea. If your dog has or has had fleas, it undoubtedly has tapeworm. A sign of infection is the appearance of segments of the worm crawling around the dog's anus or in the stool just after the dog has relieved itself. Your veterinarian can inoculate your bichon if it has this problem, and the tapeworms are quickly and completely eliminated.

Roundworms: Roundworms are not an unusual condition in dogs and are rarely harmful in an adult dog. However, these parasites can cause extreme health hazards to puppies if present in large amounts.

Roundworms can be transmitted from mother to puppies. It is wise to make sure that your female is free of roundworms before you breed her should you plan on a litter of puppies.

Heartworms: Heartworms are parasitic worms found in dogs' hearts. Dogs are the only mammals that are commonly affected. The worm is transmitted by mosquitoes that carry the larvae of the worm.

Your veterinarian can detect the presence of heartworm by a blood test. There are preventive medications for a dog that tests negative and corrective measures for the dog that has been infected.

Stings and Bites

Bichons are curious little animals and seem fascinated by all things that fly and crawl. Naturally they attempt to examine insects with their paws or mouths. This can lead to bites and stings on the foot, or worse on or around the mouth or nose.

If the sting is visible, remove it with a pair of tweezers and apply a saline solution or mild antiseptic. If the swelling is large, particularly inside the mouth, or if the dog appears to be in shock, contact your veterinarian at once.

Foreign Objects

Should you see your bichon pawing at its mouth or rubbing its mouth along the ground, immediately check to see if there is something lodged in the dog's mouth. Bichons can be intrigued by small playthings or bones and will chew and worry them until somehow they manage to get the object lodged or trapped across their teeth, usually halfway back or even at the back of the mouth where the two jaws hinge.

Should this be the case, grasp the object firmly between your fingers and push firmly towards the back of the mouth where the teeth are wider. This will usually dislodge the object, but be sure to have a firm grip on the object so the dog does not swallow it. If you are unable to remove the object quickly, get your bichon to the veterinarian at once.

If you suspect your bichon has swallowed a small ball or some other object, check to see if the object is visible in the dog's throat. If so, reach in, grasp the object, and firmly pull it out. If the dog seems to be experiencing difficulty in breathing, the object may be lodged in the windpipe. Sharp

What You Can Do if Your Bichon Is Poisoned

1. Keep the telephone number of your local poison control center with your other emergency numbers.

2. If you know or suspect which poison your dog has ingested, give this information to the poison control center when you call them. They may be able to prescribe an immediate antidote.

3. Have the emergency number of your dog's veterinarian or the nearest 24-hour emergency veterinary hospital current and easily available. Give any information you receive from the poison control center to your veterinarian.

4. If you are not sure that your dog has been poisoned or which poison it may have ingested, describe the symptoms you are observing to your veterinarian.

5. Common symptoms of poisoning: Convulsions, paralysis, tremors, vomiting, diarrhea, stomach cramps, and pains, accompanied by whimpering or howling, heavy breathing.

blows to the rib cage may cause the dog to expel air from the lungs and also expel the object.

If any small object is missing in the home and you suspect your bichon may have ingested it, do not hesitate to consult your veterinarian. An X ray will reveal the hidden "treasure" and save your dog's life.

Home Health Care

It is important to establish a weekly health care routine for your bichon. Maintaining this schedule will prevent escalation of serious problems that may take expensive veterinary attention.

Eye Care

If the eyes are inflamed or discharging any kind of matter, check for foreign bodies such as soot or weed seeds. Regular flushing of the eye with cotton and cool water will help relieve the eye of debris and pollen. However, secretion of tears and unsightly staining under the eyes can be a problem with white dogs. Have your veterinarian inspect your bichon's eyes for a condition called entropion—a condition in which the eyelid is inverted and the eyelashes cause irritation to the eye. This can be corrected by surgery.

If entropion is not the problem, bathe the eyes frequently and treat the stain by rubbing a product called fuller's earth into the stained hair while it is still wet. After it has dried, the fuller's earth should be very carefully brushed out. You can repeat this treatment regularly until the staining has been minimized. For more severe staining you may use boric acid powder in place of the fuller's earth.

Ear Cleaning

The ears should always be clean and pink. Excess hair inside the ear can create an accumulation of wax and dirt in the ear canal. This excess hair can be easily and quickly removed. Grasp a few hairs at a time with tweezers and with a quick, sharp twist and pull they will very easily discharge. Never attempt to cut hair inside the ear canal with scissors or any sharp object.

Nothing other than a cotton swab should ever be inserted into the ear itself and then never probe into the inner recess of the ear. Use the cotton swab moistened with olive or almond oil to clean the ear. If wax has accumulated, dip the cotton swab into rubbing alcohol, squeeze out the excess thoroughly and clean out the ear.

Do not attempt to treat the ear that has an unpleasant odor. Consult your veterinarian immediately.

Anal Glands

The anal glands are located on each side of the anus and should be regularly looked after. They can become blocked, causing extreme irritation and abscesses in advanced cases.

The anal glands are located on each side of the rectum. The left gland is normal but the right gland has become enlarged and needs to be emptied.

If you notice your bichon pulling itself along the ground when it is sitting down, you should check the anal glands. While not a particularly pleasant part of keeping your bichon healthy, if regularly attended to, keeping the anal glands clear is relatively easy.

The best time to attend to this job is when you are giving your bichon its bath. With the dog in the tub, place your thumb and forefinger on either side of the anal passage and exert pressure. The glands will empty quickly. Should you be unsure of how to perform this procedure, your veterinarian, groomer, or the breeder from whom you purchased your bichon will instruct you.

Dental Care

Care should always be given to the state of your bichon's teeth. If your bichon has been accustomed to chewing hard dog biscuits or gnawing on large knuckle or rawhide bones since puppyhood, it is unlikely that you will have any problems. This chewing activity assists greatly in removing dental plaque, which is the major cause of tooth decay. Any sign of redness or decay merits expert attention.

Some bichons simply do not like to chew. Should this be the case, brushing the teeth at least once a week with a good canine toothpaste will be an important part of your routine. This procedure should also be accompanied by regular veterinary checkups.

Retention of baby teeth can cause long-term problems with the permanent teeth. Generally, by the time the permanent teeth have come through at about six or seven months of age, the baby teeth have all fallen out. If there are any baby teeth remaining at this stage, seek your veterinarian's advice on their removal. Retaining baby teeth can interfere with the proper placement of your bichon's permanent teeth.

Nails

The nails of a dog who spends most of its time indoors or on grass when outdoors can grow long very quickly. Canine nail clippers are available at most pet supply shops. It is best to learn how to use these devices from your veterinarian, groomer, or the breeder from whom you purchased your bichon before you attempt to use clippers yourself.

Each nail has a blood vessel running through the center called the "quick." Cutting into the quick can be extremely painful to the dog as it contains very sensitive nerve endings. Severing the quick can also result in a great deal of bleeding that can be difficult to stop. The quick can be seen in light colored nails, but black nails make it difficult if not impossible to determine where the quick ends. When trimming the nails, especially the dark-colored nails, remove only a small portion of the nail at a time. There are any number of blood clotting products, available at

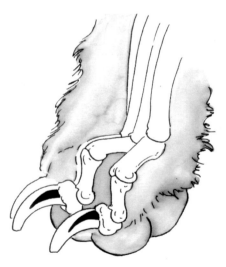

Each of a dog's nails has a blood vessel running through the center toward the end of the nail. Severing the quick can result in extensive bleeding.

Regular nail clipping keeps the nails short, reduces the possibility of cutting into the quick and avoids the nails becoming so long the foot is damaged.

pet shops, that will almost immediately stem the flow of blood should you cut into the quick.

The quick continues to grow as the nail grows. Cutting *near* to the quick causes it to recede somewhat. Therefore regular trimming will keep the quick well back from the end of the nail. You will find that the quick in neglected nails is very long and comes near to the end of the nail, making it nearly impossible to keep the length of the nail in check. You must then seek professional assistance from your veterinarian or groomer to rectify this situation.

Parasites

Fleas: While fleas are a problem everywhere and for all breeds of dogs, these pests can be especially troublesome for your bichon. In fact, some bichons are highly allergic to fleas, and the very first flea bite can set off a chain of events that can lead to what are commonly referred to as "hot spots." Hot spots are created by a dog's chewing and scratching so hard that the skin is broken. If not attended to properly the areas in which the skin

has been broken begin to form moist, painful abscesses, all hair falls away, and a veterinarian must be called upon.

As fastidious as you might be about caring for your bichon and keeping its coat in good condition, realize fleas will still be a problem. Even your bichon's daily walks can bring fleas into your home, and once there, the little creatures multiply with alarming rapidity. If you have a cat with access to the outdoors, allowing the cat in and attempting to keep the fleas out will be a next-to-impossible task. Those who live in climates in which winter temperatures drop to the freezing point will have a respite from the flea problem, but the rest of the country battles fleas year-round.

Bathing your bichon with a good flea soap or product manufactured to eliminate fleas is not enough. If you find fleas—even one flea—on your dog, there are undoubtedly hundreds of others lurking in the carpeting and furniture just waiting for your bichon to emerge from the tub so that they can hop back on.

The only way to combat fleas is to rid dog, house, and yard of the problem all at the same time. Simultaneously with your bichon's flea bath you must eliminate fleas from within your home and surrounding outdoor premises.

Flea bombs manufactured for this purpose are available at most hardware stores and veterinary offices. If your bichon never leaves the confines of your home, which is highly unlikely, using these bombs can help to correct the problem. If your bichon, like most dogs, spends any time at all in your yard or garden, you must simultaneously spray that area with a malathion or diazanon-type spray.

The best method we have found to keep the flea problem in check is for your bichon to have a flea bath at the dog-grooming salon. Arrange to have a commercial pest control service come to your home while your dog is off at the groomer. The service will spray both the interior of your home and the surrounding property as well. Most of these companies guarantee their work for a specific period of time and many offer a monthly or quarterly plan by which they will return to make sure the problem does not get out of hand again.

There is always the possibility that flea sprays and collars may be toxic to both dogs and humans. Therefore, it is very important to carefully read the instructions on the packaging of these items in order to ensure their proper use.

Fleas act as carriers of the tapeworm eggs. When a dog swallows a flea, the tapeworm eggs grow in the dog's intestines. The tapeworm is dealt with under the heading "Internal Parasites."

Lice: Lice are seldom a problem with the well-cared-for bichon, because the pests are spread by direct contact. In other words, your dog must spend time with another animal that has lice or be groomed with a contaminated brush or comb. Since these pests are minute in size they are not as easy to see as fleas, especially not on long-coated dogs.

If no fleas are present and you suspect lice, the dog must be bathed with an insecticidal shampoo every week until the problem is eliminated. Fortunately lice live and breed entirely on the dog, so it is not necessary to treat the entire area in which the dog lives.

Ticks: Your bichon can pick up ticks by running through grass, wooded areas, or even through sand at the beach. Ticks are bloodsucking insects that bury their heads firmly into the dog's skin. The tick can become a source of extreme irritation to your dog and can cause secondary infections as well. It is important to have the tick loosen its grip before you attempt to remove it. Otherwise you may allow the head to break away from the tick and remain lodged in the dog's skin. This also can create severe infections.

To remove adult ticks, soak them with a spray made especially for tick removal; once the parasite has loosened its grip you can remove it with a pair of tweezers. Regular bathing with a tick dip will prevent reinfestation. However, as is the case with all dips and sprays, read the instructions carefully as some of these products may be toxic to both you and your pet.

The entire environment in which the dog lives must be regularly and vigorously treated against ticks, especially if you live adjacent to a wooded area or beach. Ticks can transmit serious diseases that can endanger humans as well as animals. Ticks in some areas carry Lyme disease and Rocky Mountain spotted fever. It is important that you discuss the tick problem with your local veterinarian, who can advise you on which dangers might present themselves.

Helpful hint: The most common canine ailments seem to be vomiting and diarrhea. They do not mean your dog is seriously ill, but should either symptom persist, do not hesitate to call your veterinarian.

Dogs may vomit to purge their digestive tracts. Puppies may do so when they overeat or eat too much or too fast. Nervousness or fright can induce vomiting. None of this is cause for alarm unless it occurs repeatedly.

For occasional diarrhea, change from your dog's regular diet to thoroughly cooked rice with a small amount of boiled chicken added. Maintain this kind of diet until the condition improves and then gradually return your dog to its normal diet.

Inherited Problems and Diseases

Like all breeds of domesticated dogs, bichons frises have their share of hereditary problems. Probably the only dogs that do not have inherited problems, or at least do not have incapacitating problems, are wild dogs such as the dingo of Australia and the wild dog of Africa.

The major reason that wild dogs do not experience the inherited problems of their domesticated cousins is natural selection. Any genetically transferred infirmity that would interfere with the wild dog's ability to nurse as a puppy, to capture food as an adult, or to escape from a predator would automatically eliminate the individual from the gene pool.

We who control the breeding of our domesticated dogs are intent upon saving all the puppies in a litter. In preserving life we also perpetuate health problems. Our humanitarian proclivities have a down side as well.

The Bichon Frise Club of America has an ongoing committee dedicated to determining genetic disorders in the breed. Both the club and experienced breeders have literature available regarding the following breed problems and how to deal with them.

The diseases described here may not be present in the bichon you buy nor are these problems necessarily to be found in your bichon's immediate ancestors. They are breed problems, however, that should be discussed with the breeder from whom you purchase your dog. As stated previously in the chapter "Choosing Your Bichon," the reputable bichon breeder is aware of the following problems and should be more than willing to discuss them with you.

Orthopedic Diseases

Patella luxation: This condition is also commonly referred to as "slipping stifles." It is an abnormality of the stifle or knee joint leading to dislocation of the kneecap (patella). Normally the kneecap is located in a groove at the lower end of the thighbone. It is held in this position by strong elastic ligaments. If the groove is insufficiently developed, the kneecap will leave its normal position and "slip" to one side or the other of the track in which it is normally held.

The dog may exhibit an intermittent but persistent limp or have difficulty straightening out the knee. In some cases the dog may experience pain. Treatment may require surgery.

Hip dysplasia: This is a developmental disease of the hip joint. The result is instability of the hip joint due to abnormal contours of one or both of the hip joints. Some dogs might show tenderness in the hip, walk with a limp or swaying gait, or experience difficulty when getting up. Symptoms vary from mild temporary lameness to severe crippling in extreme cases. The light-bodied bichon is seldom as severely afflicted as some of the heavier-bodied breeds. Treatment may require surgery.

Eye Problems

Cataracts: This condition is a loss of the normal transparency of the lens of the eye. One or both eyes my be affected and can involve the lens partially or completely.

Some cataracts occur between the ages of one to six years and are not visible to the naked eye. These are known as juvenile cataracts. Senile cataracts occur later in life. In cases where cataracts are complete and affect both eyes, blindness results.

Corneal dystrophy: This is a condition in which there appears to be a spot (or spots) on the surface of the eye. These usually do not affect the dog's eyesight.

Progressive retinal atrophy: This condition, commonly referred to as "PRA" is a degenerative disease of the retinal cells of the eye that progresses to blindness. It usually occurs later in a bichon's life—beyond the age of six years.

Immotile Ciliary Dyskinesia

This is a defect in the microscopic hairlike structures found in various parts of the body such as the respiratory tract, uterus, testicles, and eustachian tube of the ear. This defect can cause chronic respiratory infections, sterility in both males and females, and loss of hearing.

Extensive studies continue to be done on the inherited nature of these and many other diseases. In the case of PRA, science has substantiated that the problem is inherited as a simple recessive.

To Breed or Not to Breed

Factors to Consider

We have already discussed the problem of pet overpopulation in America. A bichon owner should think long and hard before making yet another contribution to this serious situation. If you originally discussed your desire to breed your bichon with the person from whom you purchased her, that person will undoubtedly have selected a female for you that was worthy of perpetuating the breed. The operative word here of course is "worthy." Your bichon may well be cute, smart, and adore the ground you walk on, but these are not particularly good reasons for its producing offspring.

If you are unable to get in touch with the breeder of your bichon or if you doubt the credentials of the person from whom you purchased your bichon, do some research and find a breeder in your area known for producing show-quality bichons. That person is best equipped to advise you as to whether your bichon is of breeding quality. Your bichon may possess all of the qualities that make it a wonderful companion but at the same time have faults that would specifically eliminate it as a potential breeding candidate.

Most reliable breeders are quite specific when selling certain bichons that they are "pet quality only, not to be used for breeding." The "not-for-breeding" bichon will invariably be one that will be able to provide you with years of enjoyment with few if any health problems. The "not-for-breed-ing" clause is imposed by the breeder with good reason. The breeder who cares enough about the breed to make this decision will undoubtedly also be perfectly willing to discuss the reason the decision was made.

So often, people who have purchased pet bichons will come to me and say, "Ami needs to have a litter to complete her development" or "Andre needs a girl friend to relieve his frustration." Believe me, neither Ami or Andre needs sex to make life complete. In fact, in the case of Andre, breeding him will increase his frustration rather than relieve it.

Even if the caliber of the bichon you own makes it a good breeding candidate, you must consider the consequences. Males that have been used for breeding will have an extremely difficult time keeping themselves from lifting their leg and "marking" their territory. A male's territory will include your home and everything in it, including the antique sofa and Chippendale table.

Ami's litter of four will bring your canine population up to five overnight. This is no particular problem while the puppies are in the nesting box and nursing. The day will inevitably come, not too many weeks later, when Ami will wash her paws of "the gang." The puppies will very soon want liberation from the whelping box and will want to be wherever you are—*all of the time!*

Also, think back on the difficulty you experienced in housebreaking a single

If one bichon is fun, a family of five will provide five times the pleasure. Or will it? Raising a litter of puppies is something that should be considered very carefully.

bichon. Now multiply that by four and consider the cleanup involved for one (or all four).

Do realize the commitment you will have to make to being on hand when weaning time comes. Newly weaned puppies need four meals a day. Will you or a responsible member of the family be on hand to feed morning, noon, evening, and night?

Are you willing to continue to do this until you have found a good, responsible home for each puppy in the litter? This may take weeks, sometimes months, after you have already decided it is time for the puppies to be off to their new homes.

Some individuals are willing to commit to all of the above in anticipation of financial gain. They multiply the selling price of a hypothetical number of puppies by $600 to $800 and think, "Wow, what a great source of income!"

Think again! Stop to consider the cost of a stud fee and prenatal veterinary expenses. Then add the cost of possible whelping problems, health checks, and the necessary inoculation series for the puppies. These are all significant cost factors that must be taken into consideration and that will also put a very large dent in any anticipated profits.

When the Answer Is "Yes"

If what we have written thus far has not discouraged you and you have decided you really want to raise a litter of bichons, you must begin to plan well ahead. Responsible breeding is not a matter of tucking your female under your arm and heading for the nearest male of the same breed.

A tip worth considering at this point, especially if this is your first litter: a summer litter is infinitely much easier to care for than one born and growing up during seasons when the weather is inclement. The freedom to put what we refer to as our "Minnesota Wrecking Crews" safely outdoors during the summer months has proven to be a godsend, and the puppies seem to love it as well.

Think your planning through carefully. Your bichon will not whelp until approximately two months after she is bred. The puppies will spend the first four to six weeks after they are born in their whelping box. It is after that period of time that you will welcome good weather so that the youngsters can spend most of the day outdoors.

Health Checks

No bichon female should ever be bred until you are sure that she has had a minimum of two heat cycles. Prior to this time she is not completely mature mentally or physically. You must be sure she is in good health and is not a carrier for the breed's hereditary problems. Your veterinarian can assist you in determining whether the hereditary conditions exist. Some tests are fairly simple; others require X rays. Eye problems are usually diagnosed by specialists in the field.

All dogs, male and female, must be tested for canine brucellosis before being bred. This is one of the few venereal diseases that afflict dogs. It is a bacterial infection transmitted sexually and through a dog's saliva. It is one cause of abortion in females and of male sterility.

These tests for hereditary problems also apply to your male if he is to be used at stud. Again, I urge the owner of a male to consider the consequences of using the dog for breeding, even once.

Approaches to Breeding

There are three different ways of mating purebred animals of any kind. They are referred to as "Inbreeding, outcrossing, and linebreeding. The genetic inheritance of the litter your female will produce will depend upon the relationship of the individuals in her pedigree and the pedigree of stud dog you eventually select.

Inbreeding: This is an attempt to fix certain mental and physical characteristics in the offspring by mating closely related individuals. Breedings made between mother and son, father and daughter, and brother and sister are examples of inbreeding. Inbreeding fixes both qualities and faults; therefore it is a method that should be resorted to only by those completely familiar with the pedigrees and possible problems in the pedigrees of the two animals involved in the mating.

Outcrossing: Outcrossing is the opposite of inbreeding. This method of breeding mates individuals that for all intents and purposes are not related but are of the same breed. This approach is less likely to fix faults in the offspring but neither can it produce specific qualities with any certainty.

Linebreeding: This might be considered the happy medium between inbreeding and outcrossing. Related animals are used but the common ancestor or ancestors may be two or three generations removed. Linebreeding affords the same benefits and drawbacks of inbreeding, but to a lesser degree.

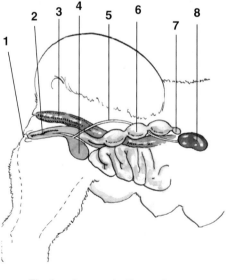

1. vulva
2. vagina
3. rectum
4. bladder
5. ureter
6. developing embryo
7. ovary
8. kidney

The female reproductive system.

Selecting the Stud Dog

The decision to breed your female was based upon the fact that she is of the quality that make her a likely candidate to produce worthy offspring. This does not mean she is a perfect bichon by any stretch of the imagination. No dog of any breed is perfect—not even the greatest show winner—and the likelihood of your bichon having no faults to compensate for in selecting a stud dog is extremely remote. The stud dog you select should excel in those areas in which your female has shortcomings.

As you read through the American Kennel Club's standard of perfection for the bichon frise you may note areas in which your female does not quite measure up. This is an extremely difficult judgment for a novice to make and it is here that the breeder from whom you purchased your female can be invaluable.

The breeder of your female will be familiar with the pedigree, the assets, and the shortcomings of the line from which your bichon descends. Your breeder will also be the best person to advise you on which faults your female has that the proper stud dog should be able to compensate for. If the breeder of your female is not available for some reason, the Bichon Frise Club of America maintains a list of responsible breeders from which you may select someone who lives nearby who may also be able to offer sound advice regarding the proper selection of a stud dog.

The Paperwork

Above all, the stud dog selected should be sound, healthy, and a typical representative of the breed. The owner should be able to present proof that care and testing indicates the stud dog is not a carrier of the hereditary problems of the breed. You should be able to provide

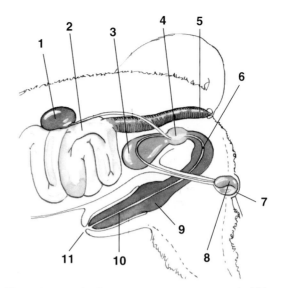

The male reproductive system.

1. *kidney*
2. *small intestine*
3. *bladder*
4. *prostate*
5. *rectum*
6. *urethra*
7. *scrotum*
8. *testes*
9. *bulb*
10. *penis*
11. *penis sheath*

proof of your female's health as well.

The stud dog owner will be able to provide you with a four-generation pedigree of the stud dog. You should also bring a copy of your female bichon's pedigree when you first go to see the stud dog. The owner of the stud will want to see if your female's bloodlines will be compatible with those of the stud. You can also ask the owner of the stud how to go about arranging to have the forthcoming litter registered.

The cost of breeding to the male you select (the stud fee) should be determined in advance as well. Stud fees vary depending upon the male's proven ability to produce quality puppies. The cost of breeding to a young male that has yet to produce a litter is going to be much less than that of a male that has produced many champion offspring. The predictability of what kind of offspring the unproven male will be able to produce is also significantly less. Again, you get what you pay for.

Summertime puppies are much easier to raise than a winter litter. Having the option of putting the puppies outdoors for part of the day is good for the puppies and a relief for the owner. This litter of puppies is ready for some outdoor fun.

The stud fee is payable at the time of breeding and is payment for breeding your female to the designated male—nothing more. The stud fee is not a guarantee of living puppies. Most breeders will give a return service as a courtesy should the female not become pregnant, but that should definitely be discussed and put in writing if the stud dog owner is agreeable to providing this return service. In fact, any agreements and conditions outside of a guarantee of actual mating should be clearly outlined in a "stud contract" or "breeding agreement."

This agreement should list the amount of the stud fee and any special conditions that apply. If the female is to remain on the premises of the stud owner while she is being bred, the contract should also state what additional costs are involved in keeping her there. The contract should state what

the owner of the stud dog is responsible for while the female is in residence.

Once the stud dog has been decided upon, the owner of the female should make a breeding reservation based upon the regularity of the female's previous seasons. This will give the owner of a popular stud dog the opportunity to schedule other females that may be coming in to breed to the dog of your choice.

It should be easy to determine from the above that the bichon male from down the street or belonging to a friend could easily be the wrong stud dog for your female. Experienced breeders have studied long and hard to learn which males and females are best suited for breeding and will advise accordingly.

The happy-go-lucky male owned by an acquaintance may carry none of the compensating qualities your female needs in her offspring. Your friend's male might conceivably even carry faults in his genetic makeup that, added to those in your female's genes, will create serious problems in the next generation.

When the Female Is "In Heat"

The female can be bred only at a particular time during her heat cycle, which lasts approximately twenty-one days. Most females will normally come into heat, called estrus, for the first time at about ten to twelve months of age. This can take place as early as six months. After her first heat your female bichon will be in heat again fairly regularly every six to eight months thereafter.

A noticeable swelling of the vulva accompanied by a dark bloody vaginal discharge is the first sign that your female is in heat. Once you have noticed this, she should be watched very carefully and kept away from all males to avoid any accidental matings. She should also be confined to an area of the household where the discharge, which she is unable to control, will not soil carpeting or furniture.

If your female is to be bred at this season you should at once notify the owner of the stud dog you have chosen. The owner of the stud dog can then schedule the breeding and tell you when to arrive with your female.

I cannot caution you enough to be extremely watchful while your female is in heat. You cannot imagine how many unwanted litters have been born even though the female was, "only with a male too young (or too old) to breed," or "in the yard by herself just a few minutes." You would be amazed at how innovative the "ready" bichon female and the "always ready" male can be when the time is right!

Normally female bichons are not ready to accept the male until about the tenth day of their heat cycle. Do not however, allow that information to lull you into believing that she *cannot* be bred until that time. While desired matings seldom are accomplished prior to the tenth day of the heat cycle, it seems *unwanted* matings are productive at almost any time the female is in heat.

Timing Is Critical

A veterinarian can be extremely helpful in advising the right day on which to breed your female. Blood tests and vaginal smears can be performed that will determine just when the female's ovulation has begun and the right time to have her bred. At this time she releases eggs that must be fertilized by the dog's sperm for pregnancy to occur. Experienced breeders and very often experienced stud dogs have an uncanny knack of being able to determine the correct day on which a female should be bred.

Even when ovulation has occurred, it may take hours or even a couple of days before the eggs are receptive to sperm. Because of the gradual ovulation, even after the first successful mating has been completed it is wise to repeat the breeding again once or twice, skipping a day between breedings to insure pregnancy.

Even though your female has been successfully mated to the dog of your choice, do not assume she cannot be impregnated by another dog. She must be closely watched until she has completely ended her heat cycle. Litters can be produced that have had two entirely different sires, one a purebred bichon, the other a dog of mixed parentage or of another breed.

None of the puppies born from a litter of this kind may be registered, as they are all of doubtful parentage. But this does not mean that your female is "tainted" for life. Her subsequent litters will not be affected in any way if she is properly mated and watched.

Pregnancy and Whelping

Is She or Isn't She?

There is nothing radically different you need do for your female bichon for the first four or five weeks after she has been bred. Maintain her normal schedule and diet. There is no reason to restrict the amount of exercise she has. In fact maintaining good muscle tone will serve her well when whelping actually occurs.

We know we cannot tell if one of our females has become pregnant for several weeks after she has been bred. Still, we invariably lapse into what we call our staring mode. While caught up in this phase we gaze intently at the mother-to-be, noting any little sign that will indicate that she is or is not pregnant. We change our minds daily, sometimes hourly, but in the end we must wait about five or six weeks, when a swelling of the female's nipples will indicate that apparently the breeding has taken.

Whelping Preparations

The gestation period is normally 59 to 63 days. That gives you plenty of time to be well prepared for the birth of the litter. One of the first orders of business should be preparing a whelping box. This whelping box will be the place where mother and offspring will spend the first several weeks of their life together.

The whelping box can be made from a cardboard shipping carton or constructed of wood. My suggestion would be to purchase or build a box constructed of wood, as the puppies will continue to use it as their bed even after they have been weaned. As the puppies grow you will find them leaving the whelping box to relieve themselves, thus assisting you in the first stages of their housebreaking.

The box should be approximately 32 to 36 inches (82–92 cm) square with sides about 8 inches (20 cm) high. The box need not be covered, but if it is, the top should be high enough to allow the mother to stand upright. Whelping boxes of various shapes and sizes can be obtained at most pet stores, or if carpentry is your long suit, a whelping box can easily be constructed of inexpensive, well-sanded wood.

Standby Whelping Equipment

Whelping box
Newsprint or newspaper
Toweling
Gauze pads
Small box with adjustable heating pad
Emergency supplemental feeder
Mother's milk replacement
Glucose
Rectal thermometer
Disposable rubber gloves
Blunt sterilized scissors
Cotton thread
Lubricant
Scale
Infrared lamp
Patience!
Telephone numbers: Veterinarian's or 24-hour emergency clinic's

The important thing is that your female be able to hop in and out of the whelping box easily without injuring her puppies. Once in, she should be able to stretch out fully on her side so that all of her nipples will be available for the puppies to nurse on. Keep the bottom of the whelping box lined with several layers of newspaper or unprinted newspaper stock. Unprinted newspaper stock can be obtained at most printing shops and will keep mother and puppies much cleaner.

Prenatal Care

As previously mentioned, there is little different that must be done for the first several weeks of pregnancy. If the female has been fed a nutritious, well-balanced diet, you need only to continue doing so.

At about the fifth week of her pregnancy her appetite will increase and you may begin to add to the amount of food she is receiving. Do not overfeed, and do not feel she must be given special food or treats. Actually, you should avoid allowing the pregnant female to become too fat. Obesity can create serious problems at whelping time. Since the female's abdomen is already crowded, several smaller meals during the course of the day will be more beneficial than allowing her to gorge herself once or twice a day.

Some dog owners feel that mega-doses of vitamins are necessary during pregnancy. This is definitely not so. In fact, many experienced breeders now feel that large doses of vitamins are dangerous, because improperly administered there can be long-range detrimental effects on a dog's skeletal development. It must be remembered that the vast majority of commercial dog foods are highly fortified to begin with, so adding high concentrations of additional vitamins without careful consideration can create problems.

This whelping box is large enough for the mother to stretch out completely making it very easy for all of her puppies to nurse.

Your veterinarian can advise you when and if any vitamins or medications are necessary. Veterinarians should also be told of your female's pregnancy prior to treatment of any kind, as no inoculations should be given that will affect the normal growth of the fetuses that she is carrying.

As the time draws near for the actual whelping, it is wise to assemble the items that will assist you in insuring that the delivery will go smoothly.

Dinner Time

Once a puppy has been dried and we are sure it is breathing properly, we allow it to nurse on the mother until contractions begin again. Among the many things with which Mother Nature has endowed the bichon, the will to survive seems high on the list. I am continually amazed at the vigor of the newborn bichon whelps and how quickly they find their mother's milk bar and commence nursing. It is only the rare bichon puppy that needs to be guided to its mother's nipple or given assistance to nurse. More often than not it is a case of insuring that the larger, stronger puppies do not push their smaller littermates out of the way and keep them from getting their fair share of milk.

While the mother is delivering a new puppy those previously whelped can rest on a heating pad in a box or basket next to the whelping box.

When the mother's birth contractions resume, we remove the previously born puppies and place them in a small box right next to the whelping box. In this way the female can see her puppies are safe as she prepares to give birth to the next one. On the bottom of the small box we have placed the electric heating pad covered with a towel. This will keep the puppies warm while they are away from the mother. It is crucial that newborn and nursing puppies not become chilled, as their temperature-regulating systems are not fully functional at this stage.

We keep water available for the female and also a bowl of broth or milk kept at room temperature throughout the whelping process. Once whelping has been completed and we have cleaned up the whelping box, we offer the nursing mother light food, such as chicken and rice or even scrambled eggs.

Veterinary Checkup

Retaining a placenta can cause serious infection. If you suspect one has been retained, mention this to your vet when you take the mother and puppies in for their general checkup. It is wise to have this checkup performed within 24 hours of whelping to avoid any complications and to make sure the mother has not retained any puppies. The vet will also inspect the puppies at this time to make sure there are no abnormalities.

This is also the time to advise your veterinarian that you will want to have the puppies' dewclaws removed. Dewclaws are the additional claws that grow slightly above the feet on the insides of both the front and rear legs. It is a good idea to have these unnecessary appendages removed, because they can become caught in a slicker brush and torn, causing injury and pain to the dog. Since bichons are brushed almost daily for their entire life, removing the dewclaws is highly recommended. We prefer to wait until bichon puppies are a few days old and have gained a little size and strength before removing the dewclaws. Done at this early age however it is literally painless and accomplished in just a minute.

Peace and Quiet

Other than the important trip to your veterinarian, the mother and puppies should be allowed as much peace and quiet as possible. Undoubtedly everyone in the household, if not the entire neighborhood, will want to see the puppies, but the mother wants and deserves privacy. Allowing her this opportunity will permit her to settle in with the important duties of bichon motherhood. Warmth and sustenance are primarily what young puppies require. A constant flow of strangers upsets the mother and disturbs the puppies.

Make sure the mother has plenty to drink at all times from now on. She must not become dehydrated.

The female's appetite will begin to increase significantly within a day or two and she should be fed several times a day, giving her as much as she wants to eat. Her regular nourishing meals should be resumed and supplemented with meaty soups and thick broths. We usually switch to puppy chow in place of the regular adult kibble, because there are more nutrients in these special formulas.

Post-whelping Complications

Bichon mothers are not generally prone to post-whelping complications, but occasionally problems do develop. It is important to be aware of the symptoms to avoid serious complications.

Mastitis: This is caused by an excess of milk in the female, causing the breasts to become hard and painful. This is common when nursing females have only one or two puppies and too much milk, with some nipples hardly used. Examine breasts regularly and massage them gently if milk is building up. If your female seems to be in pain, do not hesitate to call your vet.

Eclampsia: This is a much more serious condition but far less common than mastitis. It is caused by a shortage of calcium in the bloodstream. It may occur just before or any time after whelping, but usually at about three to four weeks after the puppies are born. Symptoms are the mother's extreme restlessness, often along with shivering and vomiting. Her legs or entire body can go stiff, and convulsions may occur. Veterinary treatment must

Getting a good start in life is important to a bichon puppy.

be sought at once. Massive injections of calcium are usually administered and recovery is normally rapid, but the mother should not be returned to her litter, as she will undoubtedly relapse.

Pyometra: Pyometra is not directly related to the birth process but occurs between mating cycles. Bacteria in the resting uterus fill it with pus. The pus causes extensive swelling and in advanced cases causes great stress on other vital organs as well. This condition can be dealt with only by a veterinarian.

HOW-TO:
Whelping

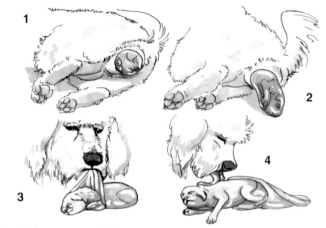

The birth sequence: **1.** Puppy appears; **2.** Comes out head first; **3.** Mother tears off placenta; **4.** Washes newborn.

Ordinarily whelping a bichon litter progresses with few complications. Nearly all of our bichons have whelped their own puppies naturally. Even first-time mothers have severed the umbilical cord and cleaned the puppies without our assistance. Our only duty has been to stand by with a watchful eye just in case complications arise.

On the rare occasion that your bichon does not respond properly or that you suspect something has gone wrong, pick up the phone and call your vet. A veterinarian is trained to know what to do and when to do it.

It is wise to be completely prepared for the female to start whelping at least a week before the time she is actually due. Some females are a few days early, others a few days late. If one of our females is running late we usually take her to our veterinarian just to make sure there are no complications.

This is not the time to allow your female to be outdoors alone for more than just a few minutes. You cannot imagine how inventive some bichon mothers-to-be can become in finding a little den under the house or some other inaccessible place to whelp her puppies. It can and does happen. Keep her in or near her whelping box as much as possible.

More than once our pregnant females have surprised us. Even though we checked to make sure whelping time was not imminent before leaving the house for a few hours, we returned to find she had commenced having her puppies.

The bichon female's temperature will usually drop from a normal of 101.5°F (38.6°C) to 99°F (37.2°C) within 48 hours of the time she will begin whelping. This is often accompanied by general restlessness, shivering, and panting.

There will often be a clear mucous discharge from the vulva that will act as a lubricant during the whelping process. The female will begin scratching in her whelping box, preparing a "nest" in which to deposit her puppies. Some females will vomit during this stage.

These signs can continue for up to 24 hours before contractions actually commence. Although it is obvious the female is experiencing discomfort, there is no need to be unduly concerned unless she appears to be in pain.

Uterine contractions increase in frequency and intensity and the vulva and vagina slowly begin to dilate. Often the laboring mother will swing around to investigate her rear end and then lie down stretching her rear legs to press against the sides of the whelping box or squat and strain as if she is trying to relieve her bowels. She may howl or whimper during these contractions.

If contractions continue and no puppies arrive during the next two hours you should definitely seek the advice of your veterinarian. In some cases a puppy is too large to be passed naturally and a cesarean section may be needed.

The First Puppy Arrives

The first puppy is usually preceded by a water bag that breaks and serves as a warning that a puppy is about to be whelped. After a few minutes and more contractions the first puppy will work its way along the birth canal and begin to emerge from the vulva, usually head first. Once the head has emerged, the female may rest a moment or two before expelling the rest of the whelp. It will be contained in a membrane sac sometimes connected by the umbilical cord to the placenta.

The puppy must be removed from the sac either by the mother or by you. Normally the mother immediately gets to work and does all that is necessary, breaking open the sac, biting through the umbilical cord and licking the puppy until it gives out a loud cry.

Some females whelping their first litter seem to be totally surprised by the arrival of their first puppy and, lacking the maternal instinct, will only look at it in amazement. It is then time for you to act. If the puppy remains in the sac it will drown and die.

Break open the membrane at the puppy's head and grasp the umbilical cord about 2 inches (5 cm) from the abdomen, draining the fluid in the cord toward the puppy. Immediately sever the cord at this point with the sterilized scissors.

Rub the puppy vigorously with rough toweling to stimulate circulation. It is wise to make sure

If the mother does not remove the membrane surrounding the puppy, break open the membrane at the puppy's head and grasp the umbilical cord about 2 inches (5 cm) from the abdomen draining the fluid toward the puppy.

that the puppy's nose and throat are clear of mucus at this time. Support the puppy in the palm of one hand with its head toward your fingers. Cover and hold the puppy securely with your other hand. Raise your arms above your head and swing the puppy downward in an arc. The centrifugal force will expel any fluids remaining in the nasal or throat passages. Newborn puppies are far less fragile than most people imagine, so do not be afraid to be vigorous in stimulating the newborn whelp. Use a drop of disinfectant to sterilize the cut end of the umbilical cord still attached to the puppy.

If the placenta has not been expelled along with the puppy, the female will normally do so shortly after the puppy is born. There is one placenta for every puppy born and they must each be accounted for. The mother instinctively wants to eat the placentas and we allow her to have one, because the placenta contains useful nutrients. Allowing her to eat them all can lead to severe diarrhea, so we quickly remove the rest as they are passed, wrap them in newspaper, and place them in the trash.

Breech Births

Barring unforeseen circumstances, the puppies will usually follow each other in irregular succession. There is no need to be concerned if the female takes time out to rest between puppies. If she continues to strain and no puppies are passed, consulting your vet is in order.

Normally puppies are born head first, but there is an occasional breech birth in which the puppy is born hind legs first.

To make sure the puppy's nose and throat are clear of mucus hold it securely between the palms of your hands with the head facing your fingers. Raise your arms above your head and swing the puppy downward in an arc. The centrifugal force will clear the puppy's airways.

There is no real need to worry about this, because as we previously stated there are no structural exaggerations in the bichon that in themselves would lead to difficult whelping. Breech births in large-headed breeds like bulldogs, Boston terriers, and the like can be difficult, because the head may not be easily passed.

We gently assist breech births if it appears necessary, especially if the breech occurs further along in the whelping process. At this point the female may be tired and the contractions not as strong. In this case all that needs to be done is to firmly grasp as much of the portion of the puppy that has emerged. As the contractions occur, simultaneously ease the puppy out. It is important to have a firm grasp on as much as possible of the puppy's body when you do this. Do not pull sharply, as the mother can be injured in this way. Should you be unable to dislodge the puppy in this manner after ten to fifteen minutes, it is best to consult your veterinarian.

Raising Puppies

Hand Rearing

Sometimes a puppy or an entire litter will have to be given supplemental feedings or be completely hand raised. There are a number of reasons that this may be necessary. At times there are individuals in the litter that are too weak to obtain the necessary amount of milk to maintain optimum growth, or the mother may not be able to nurse any of her puppies because of complications of one sort or another.

Warmth and regular feedings every two hours are critical here. A constant temperature of 85°F (29°C) can be controlled with a well-insulated heating pad in the whelping box or an infrared lamp suspended above the whelping box.

We keep mother's milk replacement and all the necessary feeding apparatus on hand prior to whelping day, just in case assistance must be given. Veterinarians are probably the best source of these items and you can get necessary instructions in how to hand feed should you have to do so.

It is very important to follow all instructions from your veterinarian and on the container that contains the feeding product. A puppy's digestive system is very delicate and can easily be upset, causing diarrhea, dehydration, and even death.

There are many different methods used by breeders and recommended by veterinarians that can be used for supplemental feeding. Discuss this issue with your veterinarian, who can not only provide you with any equipment you might need but also give you instructions on how to properly proceed with hand rearing or supplementing for a puppy or the entire litter.

Bottle Feeding

For average size newborn bichon puppies we use a baby's bottle with a baby-sized nipple for hand feeding. While the nipple may appear large, bichon puppies will learn to use these nipples quite easily. Puppies that nurse naturally on their mother suck far more than just the nipple itself into their mouths, so have little or no trouble using the baby bottle method.

Place the puppy on a rough bath towel on your lap. This surface allows the puppy to dig in with its hindquarters and gain traction, enabling it to "knead" with its front legs while it is nursing. We find using this method most closely approximates natural nursing and has been the most successful, causing the fewest problems in the long run.

Sometimes it is necessary to bottle feed puppies when the mother cannot nurse them.

Proper hand rearing and bottle feeding can result in a healthy puppy that is ready for play.

The puppy may not accept the nipple at first and you may have to gently open its mouth. Make sure the puppy's tongue is at the bottom of the mouth so that it can suck properly. It will be easier to insert the nipple into the puppy's mouth if the nipple is squeezed flat.

If the puppy does not start sucking immediately, squeeze a few drops of milk into the mouth. Usually a taste of what is yet to come will inspire most puppies to start sucking in earnest. Still, there is the reluctant pup who is bound and determined that "mom" is the only way to go, and you will have to be a bit more persistent and patient. Be sure to keep the bottle tilted at an angle so that the nipple is continually filled with milk, as you do not want the puppy to suck in air.

Newborn bichon puppies need small quantities, often. They will usually pull back and turn their heads when satisfied. As long as their abdomens seem firm and filled but not bloated, they are doing just fine. If the puppy seems gaunt and is not gaining weight, your veterinarian can properly advise you.

If you are completely taking over for the puppies' mother you will have to perform the functions the mother normally assumes. Clean the puppies mouth of any milk that has accumulated there with a piece of cotton slightly dampened with warm water. Using another swab, gently rub around the area from which the puppy urinates to stimulate it to pass water. This also must be done under the abdomen and around the anal region, encouraging the puppy to empty its bowels.

When this has been accomplished, rub these same areas with a very small amount of Vaseline to avoid chafing and irritation. This procedure must be repeated every time the puppies are bottle fed.

Obviously this procedure is going to take a significant amount of time. Hand rearing puppies is no mean feat, especially during the first two weeks when the newborn whelps must be fed every two hours. After the second week, feeding times may be spaced to two-and-a-half to three hours apart. By the end of the third week, you can begin introducing the orphans to solid food.

Use Caution

Puppies that have been nursing on their mother's milk will have derived a natural immunity from her that will last several weeks and after which they will need individual immunization. Puppies that have been completely hand raised will not have this immunity and must be protected from coming in contact with any of the airborne contagious diseases. These can be carried on the hands and shoes of almost anyone, so it is imperative to keep the puppy area as sterile as possible. Have any visiting strangers remove their shoes before entering the puppy room. We find it best not to have strangers handle the puppies at all until after the initial inoculations have been given.

Weaning

At about ten days old, most bichon puppies' eyes will have begun to open. Once all of the puppies in the litter have their eyes open weaning can commence. If the litter has been nursing on their mother right along, weaning does not necessarily have to take place this early, but at this point even the most diligent mother begins to spend progressively more time away from her puppies. Her "little angels" are rapidly developing needle-like teeth and can be quite tyrannical in having their needs met.

As this happens it is time for you to step in and offer a hand. The easi-est way to assist the transition of puppies from entire dependency upon their mother to a self-sufficient state is to allow the transition to happen gradually.

Helpful hint: Have your butcher double grind the leanest possible beef for your puppies' initial feeding. Make little balls the size of a pea from the raw meat and allow them to become room temperature. Put one of these little meat balls directly into the puppy's mouth. Some puppies get the message immediately and are ready to wolf down all the little balls you will give them. Other pups act as if you are trying to poison them and spit out your offering immediately. Even the most reluctant pup will take to the meat ball method after a day or two.

A few days later you can graduate to a small dish in which you have thoroughly moistened the finely ground cooked beef with warm milk. You can use cow's milk, goat's milk, or any one of a number of commercial brands prepared especially for dogs. In a few days granulated baby cereals can be added to this gruellike mixture and eventually well-soaked puppy chow.

Mother bichon should have some outdoor time while you are feeding the puppies or she will eat what you have put down and then regurgitate the food for the puppies. This is a natural instinct of canine mothers as their offspring come toward the end of their nursing phase and are ready to eat on their own.

It is not unusual to see a nursing mother regurgitate her own food for her puppies, especially if she is fed and then allowed to immediately return to the puppies. Most humans find this a disturbing and offensive habit, but it is not harmful to the puppies in any way unless the mother has passed back large lumps of meat or other solid food. To avoid this, it is best to keep the mother away from her puppies for at least an hour after she has eaten.

Raising the Litter

Once the puppies are completely weaned, they should learn to eat from separate dishes. While bichon puppies are a congenial sort, there could be one or two bullies who are willing to stand in the communal food pan and intimidate a more reticent littermate. Separate dishes will allow you to see how much each puppy is eating and to feed the slow eater separately if necessary. The puppies should be fed four times a day starting first thing in the morning and about every four to five hours thereafter. At least three of these meals should be semisolid food and the other one or two meals can be milk with perhaps a small amount or baby cereal of puppy kibble added.

Bichon puppies need to be treated for roundworms beginning at three or four weeks of age. Your veterinarian will prescribe the proper treatment dosage and the frequency of subsequent wormings.

While we keep strangers away from the puppies as much as possible, we encourage every member of the family to handle each puppy regularly. We have always maintained the best place for the puppy playpen is in the kitchen, where there is constant traffic and all kinds of odd noises. If there are children in the household, teach them how to play with the puppies gently. All these things will add up to a well-socialized puppy, ready to go off to its new owners and provide them with years of friendship and entertainment.

You will have done your job well.

No Business Like Show Business!

In addition to providing years of fun and companionship in and around your home, there is another aspect of owning a purebred bichon frise that you may not have considered. The bichon frise is a very popular show dog. Many owners who had thought of their bichon only as a friend and companion have entered the dog show world and found it to be an exciting and fascinating hobby. Dog shows also give competitors an opportunity to create new friendships from all walks of life and are an activity in which the entire family can participate.

The American Kennel Club sponsors many kinds of competitive events in which all registered purebred dogs may compete: conformation judging, obedience trials, agility trials, field trials, and the more recent Canine Good Citizen events.

Conformation Shows: Currently the most popular and well-attended dog events are conformation shows and obedience trials. The original purpose of conformation shows was to give breeders a means of comparing their stock to that of other fanciers and thereby make improvements in their breeding programs.

Today, not all people who participate in conformation shows intend to become breeders. Many simply find enjoyment in the competitive aspect of these events. Referred to by some as "canine beauty contests," conformation dog shows take place nearly every weekend of the year in one part of the country or another and are open to all nonneutered, AKC registered dogs.

Generally speaking, conformation shows fall into two major categories: matches and championship events. Match shows are primarily staged for the young or inexperienced dogs that are not ready to compete for championship points. In most cases classes are offered for dogs from about three months of age and older.

Match Shows

Matches are an excellent place for novice handlers to learn to show their own dogs. Since these match shows are far more informal than championship events, there is plenty of time for the novice handler to ask questions and seek assistance from more experienced exhibitors or from the officiating judges.

Match shows can be held for all breeds of dogs recognized by the AKC or they can be what are referred to as "specialty matches." The latter are for one particular breed of dog. When there is a club devoted to a specific breed in an area, that club will often hold these match shows so that the newer club members and the young puppies will have an opportunity to gain some experience.

Information regarding these matches can usually be found in the classified sections of Sunday newspapers under "Dogs for Sale." Local breeders are usually aware of upcoming events of this kind as well.

There is no need to enter these informal matches ahead of time. Most accept entries on the grounds of the show site the morning of the event. The person taking your entry will be able to assist you in filling out the entry form and give you the preliminary instructions you will need.

Championship Shows

Championship shows are much more formal and best entered after you have gained some experience by participating in several match events. Championship shows are sponsored by various all-breed kennel clubs or in some instances by a club specializing in one particular breed of dog. The American Kennel Club can provide you with the name of the all-breed kennel club in your area and the Bichon Frise Club of America can let you know if there is a bichon frise club in your vicinity. Refer to the "Useful Addresses" section at the end of this book.

How a Champion Is Made

In order for a dog registered with the AKC to become a champion, it must be awarded a total of fifteen championship points. These points are awarded to the best male and best female nonchampions in each breed. The number of championship points that can be won at a particular show is based upon the number of entries in a dog's own breed and sex entered at the show. Of the fifteen points required, two of the wins must be what are called "majors" (i.e., three or more points). These two majors must be won under two different judges.

Catalogs sold at all championship shows list the particulars relevant to every dog entered in the show. The catalog also lists the number of dogs required in each breed to win from one through five points. Since the number of dogs necessary for the various number of points differs geographically, it is important to check the catalog at each show you attend at which your male or female has been awarded points.

There are dog shows throughout the United States practically every weekend of the year. Many owners find the competitive aspect of the conformation shows extremely enjoyable and spend many weekends away showing their dogs.

How to Enter a Championship Show

All show-giving clubs must issue what is called a premium list. A premium list contains all the information you will need in order to enter that club's show. These premium lists are sent out by a professional show superintendent several weeks in advance of the closing date for entries for that show.

You must advise the show superintendent in your area that you wish to receive all premium lists for shows that will be held in your area. A list of

Dog Show Classes

Each of the following classes is divided by sex and all entries must be six months or older on the day of the show to be eligible.

Puppy class: for entries under twelve months of age on the day of show that are not champions.

12-to-18-month class: entries at least twelve months but under eighteen months of age that are not champions.

Novice class: entries born in the United States, Canada, Mexico, or Bermuda that have not prior to the closing date of entries, earned three first-place ribbons in the novice class or a first-place ribbon in bred-by-exhibitor, American-bred, or open class. Entries in this class may not have won any points toward their championships.

Bred-by-exhibitor class: entries being shown by any one of the breeders of record who is also an owner or co-owner. The entry may also be shown by a member of the immediate family of any one of the breeders of record. No champions of record are eligible for this class.

American-bred class: any non-champion entry whelped in the United States as the result of a mating that took place in the United States.

Open class: any entry six months and older.

show superintendents can be obtained from the American Kennel Club. Once your name is entered on a show superintendent's list you will continue to receive premium lists for all shows staged by that organization as long as you continue to show your dog.

The premium list will give you the date, location, and closing date for entries for a particular show. It will also list the entry fee, the judges for each of the breeds eligible to compete at the show, and the prizes that will be awarded in each breed.

Also included in the premium list is the entry form that you will need to complete in order to enter the show. All of the information you need to complete the entry form appears on your dog's AKC registration certificate. The information that you enter on this form will appear in the catalog on the day of the show.

Classes of Competition

Listed here are the classes in which you may enter your bichon at American Kennel Club shows. Read the information contained in the premium list carefully. Often there are lower rates for puppy classes as well as other exceptions that you should be aware of.

It is important to note that in dog show terminology males are referred to as "dogs" and females as "bitches." It is important to include the sex on the entry blank so that your bichon is not put into the incorrect class. It is also important to remember that while at the show, only the males are "dogs" and your cherished female will be referred to as a "bitch." Your entry will be called to the ring in that manner, so it is something that you must become accustomed to.

As you read the requirements for the various dog show classes it will become apparent that the classes are organized with respect to an entry's age and prior accomplishments. If you are a beginner we strongly advise entering your bichon in the puppy class if it is eligible. If your bichon is over twelve months of age, enter it in the twelve-to-eighteen month class. Those bichons that will have passed the eighteen-month cutoff can be entered in the novice class. Judges are far more forgiving of immaturity and lack of experience in these classes than they would be in some of the other classes that normally accommodate more seasoned dogs and handlers.

Professional handlers offer their services to those who do not wish to handle their own dog at a show or who are unable to do so. These professionals can be contacted at most dog shows. When they have completed their work for the day they are happy to discuss the possibility and the practicality of having your bichon professionally handled.

Handling Your Own Bichon

The foregoing explains the kinds of shows you may enter and how to go about doing so. Your preparation for entering shows must begin long before you actually exhibit at championship shows.

The beginner will have a great deal to learn. Much of what has to be learned is contained in books and magazine articles. Read everything that you can. Attend dog shows and observe the people in the ring with their bichons. You will quickly see how much skilled handling enhances the dog's looks and its chances of winning.

The next step is to begin to master the art of handling your own bichon. This can begin as soon as you bring your puppy home. Teaching your puppy to stand still on the grooming table while it is being brushed and combed is the initial phase of your teaching it the proper stance in the show ring.

Bichons are examined by the judge while the dog is posed on a table. This table is much like your grooming table at home; therefore it should not present a problem for your bichon. It is important that your bichon not be apprehensive when the judge attempts to examine it. You can practice staging this at home whenever strangers stop by.

There are many all-breed clubs that sponsor handling classes for people who wish to show their own dog. These classes are usually taught by professional dog handlers who will be able to offer you worthwhile tips both on handling in general and showing your bichon specifically.

In these classes you will learn a great deal about general ring procedures. At the same time your bichon will become accustomed to being handled by strangers. As you attend more and more classes you will observe your bichon growing confident and less distracted. This makes good presentation easier for both you and your dog.

While showing dogs is an enjoyable hobby, it takes hard work and a lot of study to master the art of handling your dog well. Patience and practice will help make you proficient. You will not become expert overnight.

Obedience trials: Obedience trials are held at both championship shows and matches, as are the conformation events. The same informal entry procedures that apply to conformation matches apply here as well. The

Bichons do very well in obedience competition. This hardworking bichon is pictured retrieving over a hurdle, an exercise called for in more advanced competition.

Practice makes perfect. Eventually even the novice can learn to present his or her dog well.

Bichons are always examined by the judge on a table. Here the dog is being carefully examined by the judge in the show ring.

championship or "sanctioned" obedience trials are normally held in conjunction with conformation events and require pre-entry. They are handled in a more formal manner.

Obedience classes are definitely prerequisites here, since competition is highly precise and based entirely upon your dog's performing a set series of exercises. The exercises required in the various classes of competition range from basics like heel, sit and lie down in the novice class through the sophisticated exercises of the utility and tracking dog levels that require scent discrimination and directed jumping.

Each level has a degree that can be earned after attaining qualifying scores at a given number of shows. The competition levels and corresponding degrees are: Novice, earning a Companion Dog degree (CD), Open, which earns the Companion Dog Excellent degree (CDX), Utility, earning the Utility Dog and Utility Dog Excellent degrees (UD and UDX). Tracking events earn the rare Tracking Dog and Tracking Dog Excellent titles (TD and TDX).

Undoubtedly because of their trick and circus dog heritage, bichons have proven to be excellent candidates for obedience titles. Many have achieved their Companion Dog and Companion Dog Excellent degrees through the years and the breed is proud to claim title holders in even the most demanding of the categories.

Agility: Agility competition is for all intents and purposes an obstacle course for dogs. Everyone involved (and everyone who watches) appears to be having the time of their lives. There are tunnels, catwalks, seesaws, and numerous other obstacles that the canine contestants must master off leash while being timed. Still in the early stages of growth, this event is catching on rapidly and will undoubtedly become one of the biggest attractions at all-breed dog shows.

Noncompetitive Pursuits

Canine good citizen test: Though this event does not achieve any AKC title it is nonetheless an extremely valuable accomplishment. The purpose of the test is to demonstrate that the canine entered is well mannered and an asset to the community. There are ten parts to the test and the dog must pass all ten in order to be awarded a certificate. The ten parts are

1. Appearance and grooming
2. Acceptance of a stranger
3. Walking on a loose leash and heel
4. Walking through a crowd
5. Sitting for examination
6. Sitting and lying down on command
7. Staying in both the sit and down position
8. Positive reaction to another dog
9. Calm reaction to distracting sights or noises
10. Dog can be left alone (tied with leash while owner is out of sight)

Therapy Dogs

Bichons have also proven themselves admirably as therapy dogs. This is a field in which dogs are trained to assist the sick, the handicapped, and the aged. Because bichons have a long history as companions and are of an easy-to-handle size, they are particularly suited to this work.

Bichons can be trained in a wide range of assistance roles. Their keen vision and hearing make them ideal companions for the hard-of-hearing and the sight-impaired, warning their

This bichon is pictured in obedience competition leaping over the hurdles.

owners of situations or sounds that the handicapped might not be capable of recognizing.

An organization called Therapy Dogs International registers dogs that are temperamentally suitable to visit hospitals and homes for the aged. It has been found that there is great therapeutic value to the patients who come in contact with these dogs. Medical journals have substantiated stress reduction and lowered blood pressure as a result of these human to animal associations. Bichons, being the clowns that they are, add an element of humor and entertainment to the comfort they bring.

The Bichon Frise Club of America, the American Kennel Club, or your local obedience club can provide you with information regarding Therapy Dogs International.

Useful Addresses and Literature

International Kennel Clubs

Bichon Frise Club of America
  Mrs. Bernice Richardson
  186 Ash St. N.
  Twin Falls, ID 83301

American Kennel Club
  51 Madison Avenue
  New York, NY 10010
  Tel. (212) 696-8200
  All Registration Information:
  American Kennel Club
  5580 Centerview Drive
  Raleigh, NC 27606
  Tel. (919) 233-9767

Australian National Kennel
Council
  Royal Showgrounds
  Ascot Vale 3032
  Victoria, Australia

Canadian Kennel Club
  89 Skyway Avenue, Unit 100
  Etobicoke, Ontario
  Canada M9W 6R4
  Tel. (416) 675-5511

The Kennel Club
  1-5 Clargis Street
  Piccadilly, London W1Y 8AB
  England

New Zealand Kennel Club
  Private Bag 59003
  Porirua, Wellington
  New Zealand

United Kennel Club
  100 E. Kilgore Road
  Kalamazoo, Michigan 49001-5598

Periodicals

Bichon Frise Reporter
  P.O. Box 6369
  San Luis Obispo, CA 93412

Dog Fancy
  P.O. Box 6050
  Mission Viejo, CA 92690
  Tel. (800) 426-2516

Dog World
  29 North Wacker Drive
  Chicago, IL 60606
  Tel. (312) 726-2802

Dogs In Canada
  Apex Publishers
  89 Skyway Ave. #200
  Etobicoke, Ont.,
  Canada M9W 6R4

AKC Gazette
  51 Madison Avenue
  New York, New York 10010

Books

Sabella, Frank. *The Art of Handling Showdogs.* Hollywood, California: B & E Publications, Inc., 1980

Stubbs, Barbara. *The Complete Bichon Frise.* New York, New York: Howell Book House., 1990

Beauchamp, Richard G. *The Bichon Frise Today.* North Hollywood, California: Rohman Publications., 1982

Beauchamp, Richard G. *Bichon Frise Workbook.* North Hollywood, California: Rohman Publications., 1975

Beauchamp, Richard G. *The Bichon Frise Handbook.* North Hollywood, California: Rohman Publications., 1972

Smythe, R.H. *The Breeding and Rearing of Dogs.* New York, New York: Arco Publishing Company, Inc., 1969

Ransom, E. Jackie. *The Bichon Frise.* H. London, England: H.F. & G Witherby, Ltd., 1990.

Colflesh, Linda. *Making Friends (Training Your Dog Positively).* New York, New York: Howell Book House., 1990

Squire, Dr. Ann. *Understanding Man's Best Friend.* New York, New York: Macmillan Publishing Company, 1991

Index